Our Father

Our Father
Discovering Family

Mitch Carnell

Foreword by
Thomas R. McKibbens

RESOURCE *Publications* • Eugene, Oregon

OUR FATHER
Discovering Family

Copyright © 2015 C. Mitch Carnell, Jr.. All rights reserved. Except for brief quotations in critical publications or reviews, no part of this book may be reproduced in any manner without prior written permission from the publisher. Write: Permissions. Wipf and Stock Publishers, 199 W. 8th Ave., Suite 3, Eugene, OR 97401.

Resource Publications
An Imprint of Wipf and Stock Publishers
199 W. 8th Ave., Suite 3
Eugene, OR 97401

www.wipfandstock.com

ISBN 13: 978-1-4982-1873-3

Manufactured in the U.S.A.   05/19/2015

To my sister, Jean Carnell Wallace, and my grandchildren, Christopher, Christina, and Colin.

I will lead the blind by paths they have not known,
Along unfamiliar paths I will guide them;
I will turn the darkness into light before them
and make the rough places smooth.
These are the things I will do;
I will not forsake them.

—ISA. 42:16 (NIV)

Contents

Foreword by Thomas R. McKibbens | ix
Preface | xiii

1. Discovery and Reflection | 1
2. Woodruff and Northside Baptist Church | 6
3. Off to College | 15
4. Beyond the Ivied Walls | 29
5. Marriage—The Liz Factor | 33
6. Home at Last | 44
7. Hard Lessons | 48
8. My Darkest Hours | 54
9. Surrender | 64
10. New Beginnings | 67
11. Playing God and Failing Miserably | 71
12. Grace upon Grace | 77
13. Friends and Mentors | 93
14. Autumn | 82

Bibliography | 97

Foreword

AUTOBIOGRAPHY AT ITS BEST is a moving, quivering love that is written with tears and great laughter. Those tears and that laughter inevitably work their way into the neurons of the brain, and if one is fortunate, into the depths of a person's heart. When that happens, there is an unbreakable link between the writer and the reader. You can sense that link as you read the work of Mitch Carnell, for his experiences chronicled here are not just personal; they are universal. I have always thought that it takes a great deal of courage and even gall to write an autobiography. To expose oneself to such public view might be considered an act of hubris by some; but there is none of that in these pages. This account is filled with the fragrance of genuine humility. It is a gift to those who know Mitch Carnell; it is sheer benediction to anyone who ventures past the first sentence.

For a Southern Baptist who has spent most of his life in South Carolina and lived in a city that many would consider the most southern of all the cities in the south, it is startling that his account begins not in the south at all, but in London, in the middle of St. Paul's Cathedral, on a busy day when the church was filled with tourists from all over the world. In a way, that is a perfect picture of the life Mitch Carnell describes. It is a life in which church plays a central role, but his is a world church, a church welcoming all kinds of people from all kinds of places. His church is as expansive as the love of God he describes in his experiences, and at the same time as practical as a local church deacons' meeting.

I first met Mitch Carnell when (seemingly right out of the blue) he called me early in the 1990s to ask if I would be interested in giving the Hamrick Lectures at the First Baptist Church in Charleston. I jumped at the chance, for at the time I had never visited Charleston or had the chance to visit that historic church, which had been founded by a group from the First Baptist Church of Boston in the 17th century, making it the oldest Baptist church in the South, and linking it historically to New England. Besides that, I was descended from one of its pastors, Basil Manly, Sr. When Mitch asked me how much I would charge for the lectures, I almost blurted out that I would pay him to give those lectures!

The experience of meeting Mitch Carnell in person left a deep and lasting impression on me. I immediately knew that he was a man of depth and integrity, a person who was serious about things that mattered, but not so full of himself that he couldn't share a great laugh. He was, in short, a delight to meet and know. Our friendship was sealed after those lectures, and it has only grown over the years. These chapters help me know him on an even deeper level. His writing is honest and frequently profound.

But there is something deeper in this book than getting to know Mitch Carnell as a person. Within these pages you will find a spiritual journey, at times reveling on the mountaintop and at times trudging along the deepest valley. You will likely find yourself somewhere along his journey, and you will join him on a pilgrimage that Christians of every age and every denomination have experienced. His wisdom along the way is deeply moving and helpful.

This is not a Southern Baptist book, but it is a book about a Southern Baptist. He describes his travels as a committed lay church leader through the thickets of denominational controversy, the indescribable pain of personal loss, and the sheer joy of deep friendships. In short, he is a master of describing life as he has experienced it, and he inevitably pulls the reader in to share that life with him.

Foreword

A note about the title of his book: it is a reference to the prayer known throughout the world as the "Our Father," or the "Lord's Prayer." Diving deeply into this pool of depth and inspiration, you will come up after reading it with a renewed sense of the "Our" in the prayer, and you will know that you, too, are included in that word!

—Thomas R. McKibbens

The Rev. Dr. Thomas R. McKibbens is the Interim Pastor of the First Baptist Church of Providence, Rhode Island, the first Baptist Church in America. He is the author of *The Forgotten Heritage: A Lineage of Great Baptist Preaching* (Mercer University Press. 1986). He is writing a history of the First Baptist Church of Boston.

Preface

THIS IS MY STORY as seen through my eyes as I pursued my quest to understand my journey of faith. That journey has brought me full circle back to where I started as a child at Northside Baptist Church. God is love. These three little words have exploded in meaning far beyond my childhood understanding. They have expanded to include all of humanity and God's creation. My quest experienced a major jolt from my experience at St. Paul's Cathedral in London and the recitation of the "Our Father" prayer by hundreds of fellow tourists.

Joe Chris Robertson, my art professor at Mars Hill University, told me, "Mitch, I want to know how you see this through your eyes." My sister, Jean, my wife, or my children, Suzanne and Michael, could tell my story, but it would be their interpretation, not mine. I take full responsibility for what I have written. I have done my best to be an honest reporter; however, what you remember and how you remember it may not be how I remember it, and we are both right.

I enjoyed an enormously satisfying career as President/CEO of the Charleston Speech and Hearing Center. My life at Charleston's historic First Baptist Church has brought wonderful people into my life. Dr. John A. Hamrick challenged me to go full throttle in exploring my faith. David Redd, Minister of Music and Worship, thrilled my soul with his classical church music and remarkable devotion to worship.

Preface

Rev. Marshall Blalock is a source of support and encouragement. He graciously shouldered much of the criticism for the choice of speakers at the Hamrick Lectureship and for his endorsement and promotion of the Say Something Nice Sunday Movement. Lori Lethco, his administrative assistant, has aided me in so many ways with her abundant talents and skills, which she has dedicated to God.

Dr. Monty Knight, Carl Tolbert, Bob Boston, Dr. Tom Guerry, Phil Bryant, Bruce Jane, and John Hughes are all ministers and are trusted Christian mentors and friends. Sister Sandra Makowski has expanded my appreciation for the importance of acts of kindness in our daily journey. She could have used Rev. Gene Plyler as an example of kindness and caring in her book. Ann Fox, whose father was both a Baptist and Presbyterian minister during the Great Depression, brightens my life every Sunday morning, and she is a breath of fresh air. Ann was the director for our wedding when Carol and I married. Obviously she did a great job. Jane Hamrick is a source of strength, encouragement, kindness, and humor. Her insights into all things Baptist are extremely valuable in helping me to understand many different viewpoints.

I owe a great debt to my parents. who. through their example. set me in the right direction. My sister, Jean, has the greatest capacity for love of anyone I know. The members of Northside Baptist Church loved me, encouraged me, and gave me a sound foundation. I can never repay the debt I owe Furman University and especially Sara Lowrey for what I gained there. Drs. T. Earle Johnson and Ollie Backus at the University of Alabama influenced my life greatly. Drs. Waldo Braden and George Gunn at Louisiana State University modeled for me what a true professional really looks like in his or her dealings with others.

My late wife, Liz, was the most accepting and kindest person I have ever known. Carol, my second wife, gave me my life back after Liz's much too early death. My children, Suzanne and Michael, are constant fountains of love, joy, and challenge.

I am grateful to my friend, Dr. Tom McKibbens, for agreeing to write the Foreword to my book. I became a fan, and he

Preface

became a mentor, when he spoke to the John A. Hamrick Lectureship in Charleston. In my mind he embodies the very best of our Baptist heritage of thinking, reasoning, compassionate, involved Christians.

I am indebted to Diane Dill for her work as copy editor, which has made this much more readable. Most of all I want to thank her for her words of encouragement.

There are so many others that I should name, but the list would be too daunting. They are all gifts that God has brought into my life.

All of our experiences provide avenues for understanding ourselves, helping others, and glorifying God. Every circumstance contains the potential for growth. As I have struggled with writing this over the past few years, I have grown in my understanding of who God is and who belongs in his/our family.

—Mitch Carnell
Charleston, South Carolina

1

Discovery and Reflections

"London—what a romantic and exciting place to go on our honeymoon!" Carol announced, catching me by surprise. The only place she had ever talked about wanting to visit was Hawaii. It never occurred to me to suggest London. I could hardly contain my enthusiasm. Going to London would be the fulfillment of a lifelong dream—an answer to prayer. I don't know when or why her change of heart took place. Her only explanation was that we would be living in Charleston, South Carolina, near the ocean and could visit the beach anytime.

Carol grew up in a very poor family in a decaying section of Huntington, West Virginia. She had virtually no travel experience and little organized church experience. I grew up in a cotton mill village in upper South Carolina and have been in church all of my life. This is a second marriage for both of us. Carol's first marriage ended in bitter divorce after twenty years, and my Liz died unexpectedly of an aneurysm after thirty-two years of marriage, long before her time. Carol and I dated (strange term for people our age) for seven years.

After fabulous trips to Stonehenge (Carol's favorite), Bath, Stratford-on-Avon, Oxford, Edinburgh, Cardiff, a dinner cruise on the Thames, and strolling the streets of London, we saved the last full day of our honeymoon for touring Buckingham Palace and Westminster Abbey—not a very savvy decision. After a much longer walk than we expected from the Big Red Bus stop, we discovered that the lines at the Palace were too long for any reasonable expectation of getting in. Disappointed not to get inside, we saw as much as we could see, enjoyed the park, and reluctantly moved on.

The same story greeted us at Westminster Cathedral. We again saw as much as we could possibly see. We tarried awhile just to soak it all in and promised ourselves that we would come back on our tenth anniversary. We headed for St. Paul's Cathedral. This time we were smart enough to go by taxi, which was an adventure itself.

I believe that some things are pre-ordained. Although St. Paul's was crowded, we managed to get inside. What a breathtaking, soul-stretching, holy place! We were simply overwhelmed by its beauty and grandeur. Every step revealed a new treasure. Neither of us had ever experienced anything that came remotely close to this. Every nerve in my body tingled with the sheer majesty of it all, and I could hardly believe I was here. All of the guidebooks put together could not prepare one for this. How could anyone possibly digest it all? As magnificent as the cathedral is, and as elated as I was to be there, my real epiphany was yet to come.

At 11:00 a.m. the public address system came on. The priest introduced himself and then said, "At this time each day we pause and say together the 'Our Father' prayer."

Then the most unbelievable thing happened. Voices belonging to people from around the world, of every language, of every color and hue, every nationality, handicapped and whole, male and female, child and adult, gay and straight, prayed aloud together, "Our Father."

For the first time in my sixty-five years, the full meaning of the opening words caressed my soul in a way I had never experienced before. Here in this ancient house of worship, in this ancient city with my new bride, the true meaning of "Our Father" coursed through my veins. I was awestruck. There was no turning back. It was the beginning of a new understanding of my journey of faith. I could hardly contain the sensation of oneness in God that engulfed my entire being. I knew that my understanding of God had taken a quantum leap. "Our" took on a meaning far greater, far more profound, than its three characters would signal. This must

Discovery and Reflections

be what Saint Paul had felt on the road to Damascus. "Who are you Lord?" Saul asked. "I am Jesus, whom you are persecuting" Acts: 9:5 (New International Version).

As I struggled to comprehend this unexpected revelation and gain some perspective, my thoughts drifted back to my childhood. Incidents and experiences that had remained separate and unexplored for their meanings for all of these years began to come together, and a pattern began to emerge. Two years later, I discovered a prayer by Pam Kidd in *Daily Guideposts 2001* that expresses the same phenomena that God can take a life that is in pieces and put it together according to his plan[1] The pieces of my life were slowly coming together. I understood that my revelation at St. Paul's is not the result of an isolated incident; rather, it had been a lifetime in the making.

In Dr. Scott Walker's book, *Understanding Christianity? Looking through the Windows of God*, he puts it this way: "We can not know anything about God—even discern God's existence—unless God chooses to reveal God's self to us."[2] God was certainly opening a window for me.

My friend, Dr. Monty Knight, introduced me to perhaps the best summation of what I was experiencing, with a passage from *The Quest for the Historical Jesus* by Albert Schweitzer.

> He comes to us as one unknown, without a name, as of old, by the lakeside, he came to those who knew him not. He speaks to us the same word: 'Follow thou me!', He commands and sets us to the tasks which He has to fulfill for our time. And to those who obey Him, whether they be wise or simple, He will reveal Himself in the toils, the conflicts, the sufferings which they will pass through in His fellowship, and, as an infallible mystery, they shall learn in their own experience who He is.[3]

This was my time, a time for the pieces of my life to come together. What grand design had brought me to this point?

1. Kidd, *Daily Guideposts 2001*, 22.
2. Walker, *Understanding Christianity?*, 8.
3. Schweitzer, *The Quest of the Historical Jesus*, 401

Our Father

While my grandmother Carnell was living, my dad's side of our family held annual family reunions. These were great affairs with aunts, uncles, cousins, and friends. The food was unbelievable because all the aunts competed with one another, and each one had her own specialty: country ham, fried chicken, roast turkey, cornbread dressing, ambrosia, sweet potato soufflé, potato salad, apple pie, peach cobbler, pineapple-upside-down cake, pecan pie, German chocolate cake, and beans of every description. If you had confronted the aunts with this fact, they would have denied its truth, but I knew which offering to head for first before it was scooped up by others. None came close to equaling my mother's fried chicken and made-from-scratch biscuits. Hers were simply the best. Unfortunately, I didn't appreciate these gatherings then as I do now. How I wish I had paid more attention.

Some of my earliest memories are of Northside Baptist Church, a mill village church in Woodruff, which was a few doors diagonally across from our house. We had a wonderful pastor, Roy R. Gowan, whom we called Preacher Gowan. He and my dad were the best of friends and he was in our home often. It was only natural for Dad to invite him to the family reunion under the great spreading oak trees at Aunt Sally Lou Hanna's house. It was just as natural for him to ask Preacher Gowan to return thanks before the meal. At one of our gatherings, as soon as Preacher Gowan said, "Let us bow our heads and close our eyes," my Great Aunt Anna Brown said in a loud voice, "How are we supposed to eat with our heads down and our eyes shut?"

At that moment, had he possessed the power, my dad would have deleted Aunt Anna right out of our family. I had never seen him so embarrassed. I never thought of this incident again until this visit to St. Paul's.

Years later we were at the wake for my Uncle Calvin. I was sitting with several of my aunts, my sister, and a few cousins. Somehow the conversation got around to my Uncle Jack, who had died a few years before. One of my aunts had a vicious tongue, and she said about his widow, who was one of my favorites, "Well, Jack is dead. She's no longer part of our family." Her pronouncement horrified everyone present. Then, as now, someone or some group is always trying to get rid of part of God's family. Some group is always trying to establish a set of rules that will exclude those they do not like. They strive to make the Bible say something that it does not say. Dr. Tom Guerry tells the story about a member of his former congregation in Morganton, North Carolina, who would often ask, "That's in the Bible, isn't it, preacher?"

"No!" Tom would say, "I don't believe it is."

"Well," his friend would add, "If it isn't, it ought to be."

As I stood in St. Paul's during that most reverent of moments, these long forgotten memories flooded over me. I could hardly cope with my revelation. Never before had I paid any attention to the significance of that little word in "Our Father." Never again would I be able to ignore it. "*Our*" is a powerful word.

What I am learning as the message at St. Paul's continues to seep in is that there are no limitations on who can call upon God. To paraphrase Revelation 22:17 (NIV), "Whosoever will, let him/her come." Before this revelation, "whosoever" was just another one of those fly-by words—like *"our."*

2

Woodruff and Northside Baptist Church

IN THE TIME JUST after the Second World War, Woodruff, South Carolina, was not an ideal place to learn about the brotherhood of man. We were a small provincial cotton mill town seventeen miles from the nearest city of any significance. The returning GIs did begin to change things. They had seen the outside world, and they came home different from when they left. Uncle Jack came back from Europe with a much broader outlook than anyone I knew. Many of his new viewpoints were soundly rejected by the other adults. Even though I was just a boy, he and I had long discussions because I listened to him. I was absolutely fascinated by his adventures. He rarely discussed the fighting, but he did tell me about the places and people. Most of all, I knew that I agreed with what he said. He was my hero. In my childlike way, I realized that the world was somehow different outside my little part of it, and he ignited in me the desire to find out for myself. That spark has never been extinguished.

There were clues along the way of what was to come, but I was either too young or too naive to understand them. Dad worked at the Woodruff Auto Supply Company after debilitating asthma forced him to leave the dust of the cotton mill. When I was in the seventh grade, a mechanic came into the store one morning, covered with grease. He asked my dad for the price of a particular item. Dad gave him the price. The man thanked him and left.

"I guess he can't afford that," I chuckled.

"Do you know that man?" my dad asked sternly.

"No, sir."

"Do you know anything about him?"

"No, sir."

"Then how do you know what he can afford and what he can't? He might be here to compare prices. His boss could have sent him. He might be coming back later to buy it. You don't know anything about that man."

What a lesson, even though it took me years to figure it out.

Dad liked to tell stories, and one of his, and my, favorites was about a black sharecropper, to whom everyone referred as "Old John." Year after year Old John brought his bales of cotton to be ginned. Year after year the story was the same. Mr. Jim, the owner of the cotton gin house would say, "John, you almost did it this year. If you had just one more bale of cotton, you would be in the black and have some profit."

John would thank Mr. Jim and vow to do better. At this point in the story, my dad's face lighted up and a smile came into his voice.

"This year John showed up with his cotton bales, and Mr. Jim repeated the familiar words, "John, you almost made it. If you had just one more bale of cotton, you would be in the black and make a profit."

"I've got it, Mr. Jim!" Old John exclaimed as all the other men in the gin house broke into gales of laughter. Mr. Jim was speechless. Everyone knew what had happened. Mr. Jim had been cheating Old John for years. This time Old John had gotten the better of him.

My dad identified with Old John, with the underdog. He always sided with what was right. He was not only teaching me about fairness, but he was also setting a Christian example. I had to be an adult before I would understand all of the contradictions I witnessed while growing up. Many people claimed Christianity, yet their words and behavior did not always bear this out.

As children at Northside Baptist Church, we sang, "Jesus loves the little children of the world—brown and yellow, black and white. They are precious in his sight. Jesus loves the little children of the world."[1]

Somehow we managed to blot out the children down the street and to think of "the little children of the world" as being in Africa or China. From the earliest age, we contributed our pennies for missions for those far-off children. One incident is seared into my memory, and it will not fade with time. One Sunday morning when I was in the second grade, two black children showed up for Sunday school. They were not turned away, but they were seated over by the door, away from the rest of us. They could only watch and did not enter into any activities. I never saw those two children again, nor did I ever hear any adult discuss the occurrence of the children's visit or the way they were treated. The lessons were there, but no one helped us make the application except, perhaps, Preacher Gowan. He told me one day, "Mitchell, God made all of you, including your brain. He didn't expect you to park it at the door when you come to church. There's nothing wrong with honest questions." At the time, I had no way of knowing what a gift Preacher Gowan had given to me. Looking back now, I know this was one of the defining moments of my life. Perhaps it is the most valuable gift I have ever received. It freed me to question, to ponder, to grow.

A giant influence in my life at this time was our next-door neighbor, Mrs. Elma McGill. I called her Miss Elma. She and her husband, Mr. Andy, were the leaders of the RAs (Royal Ambassadors—a mission study group for young Baptist boys). Several boys met at their house once a month for a devotional time, games, and desserts. Even though I was too young to be part of the group, I was always included. "I'm not going to have all these other boys over here and not invite Mitchell," Miss Elma said. She encouraged me in everything I tried. She remained one of my chief boosters until she died. The last time I visited her, she rummaged around

---

1. Woolston, Clare Herbert (lyrics) and George Root (music), *Jesus Loves the Little Children*, 1800s.

in her closet until she found a box of Girl Scout cookies to give to me. She never stopped giving. I was humbled to be asked by her children to deliver her eulogy. She loved me, and I knew it. It was never spoken, but it was unconditional. I thought of her as a second mother. By example, she taught me to include people. I know that now. She was certainly one of the building blocks for my growing understanding of who God is and who is in his family.

In the sixth grade, there was a girl in my class whose family was obviously poorer than the rest of us. There were no hot school lunches in those days, only cold sandwiches, milk, and fruit. Mary never had a lunch. When I told my parents about Mary, they sent the money for her lunches. I was not surprised. I didn't know where they would get the extra money; I only knew that they would. I took lots of teasing about Mary being my girlfriend, but I knew that I had done the right thing.

We were in church one Sunday night, and it came time for the offering. I turned to my dad and said, "I don't have an envelope for my money. They won't know who gave it."

"God knows," he said.

On one of those very rare occasions when all four of us [Mom, Dad, my sister, Jean (short for Imogene), and I], were in Spartanburg, Dad gave me a quarter for shopping just as we approached a street beggar. Naturally I promptly dropped my quarter into his box. The surprised reaction from Dad let me know that I had made a mistake, but he didn't say anything. Quarters were hard to come by, but even though his first reaction was one of surprise, I felt that he was pleased with my generosity. Most of his lessons were like that. He didn't preach. He left it to me to think these lessons through.

The radio evangelist, J. Harold Smith, grew up in our church and began his preaching career there. Although he got his start there, he offended so many of the members that he was never invited back to preach. My friend Bobby Allen and I attended the camp that Smith owned in North Carolina—Camp Pisgah. J. Harold Smith preached hell fire and brimstone. He told story after story about drinking, gambling, and womanizing. Neither of us had ever heard that kind of preaching before, nor did we know anything about womanizing. I asked Preacher Gowan when he was going to tell us his story about drinking, gambling, and womanizing. "Mitchell, I thank God every day that he saved me from those types of experiences," he said, matter-of-factly.

For several consecutive Saturday mornings when I was eleven years old, Preacher Gowan gathered several of us pre-teens together to talk with us about accepting Jesus as our personal savior and what that meant. All of us had been in church all of our young lives, and all of us were from Christian homes. It had probably never occurred to us not to believe. It was really more of making it official. Preacher Gowan applied no pressure, and neither did our parents. Either Mother or Dad asked both Jean and me why we wanted to become Christians. Our answers must have been satisfactory. The following Sunday morning while the congregation sang, "Just As I Am." I made my profession of faith official. Even today, I get cold chills and a wonderful feeling when I hear that magnificent old hymn. The old hymns have always had a hold on me. Elizabeth McGill played the electric organ at Northside, and her playing always spoke to me, especially when she played the bells. When I broke my collarbone by falling after hanging upside down in a peach tree, aunts and uncles gave me nickels and dimes to make me feel better. I used them to buy a copy of the little red paperback songbook that my age group was using. I can still almost make out the title in my mind's eye. It had black lettering on a dark red cover.

Northside Baptist Church was a wonderful place filled with loving, caring people who only wanted the best for their children. I know the foundation I received in that fellowship has allowed me to explore my faith. Those wonderful people encouraged me and all of the other young people in everything we did. I was in the Christmas plays, spoke in Sunday school, and later delivered the message during Youth Night at Christmas. The now-defunct Baptist Training Union provided great opportunities to learn and practice our speaking and discussion skills. Northside Baptist Church will always have a special spot in my heart. If I close my eyes, I can still see myself sitting on the front row as a young boy or further back on the right hand side as a teenager. I can see the Christmas tree and the Santa Claus who gave presents to everyone, from the youngest to the oldest.

In those days teenage boys who were active in church life received a lot of encouragement, if not downright pressure, to become a preacher. Naturally I talked to Preacher Gowan about this. "Mitchell," he said, "as long as you can be happy and do anything else, then don't do it. If you reach a point in your life where you can't be happy doing anything else, then become a minister of the Gospel."

There was no doubt in my mind that this was the best advice I would ever get on this topic. I knew that he loved me and wanted the very best for me. Later, he left Woodruff for Union and then Greenville, South Carolina. While I was a student at Furman University, Pastor Gowan invited me to speak at the Wednesday night prayer service at his church. I had no way of knowing how much this man had influenced my life. Today, I try to use this story of Preacher Gowan to encourage several of my minister friends, who often are discouraged by the lack of outward responses to their messages. I wish Preacher Gowan could have known the influence that he would have on my life, just as I wish today's ministers could realize the influence they are having on the lives of others. They are planting seeds that may take decades to grow. I was perhaps twenty-one years old the last time I talked with Preacher Gowan, but he is never far from my mind. When I realize how different my religious training could have been growing up when and where I did, my gratitude to this wonderful man knows no bounds. He freed me to think, explore, and grow without guilt. He assured me that my questioning nature was not an affront to God, nor did it displease him. I can easily picture Preacher Gowan's study today, and I can still hear his quiet, calm, reassuring voice. He always had time for me, and I spent many hours with him. He assured me that God loved me and that nothing could ever change that.

Lightning struck that summer. I got my first glasses that allowed me to read normal size print for the first time. They had telescopic lens for my right eye. "Ugly" is too mild a word to describe them, but "wonderful" is far too weak to describe their impact. I still had to hold a book close to my face, but I could read it. Dr. Parks, an optometrist, opened an office in Woodruff two days a week, and he labored hard to help me. I would not wear them in public, but neither would I be without them.

I had never ridden on a train, nor had I been on any kind of long trip without my parents. In the eleventh grade, I had the opportunity to represent our Future Farmers of America chapter at the national convention in Kansas City. Our chapter won a coveted national award, and I would go to accept it on behalf of our chapter. Boys from all of the chapters in South Carolina shared a train car, and we added other state cars as our train moved toward Kansas City. There was a mass of boys and faculty when we reached the convention center. Here were boys from all over the country. Many were from places smaller than, and just as provincial as, Woodruff, but we had competed successfully on a national level.

I was impressed with everything from seeing the high water marks at Swift and Company from the recent flooding, to the grain elevators, to the latest farm equipment, to our magnificent hotel, the Town House, which had just opened. My world was expanding. Once again my parents found the money so that I could have this experience. Even more important, they summoned the courage to allow me to do it. I know now how much they worried about how I would get around with my poor eyesight, but they wanted me to not miss out on anything and to become as independent as possible. Over and over again, they managed to subdue their desire to protect me so that I could experience the real world. I realize now how Mother suffered over the ridicule I often encountered because of my snow white hair and pale complexion. Letting me experience life never ceased to be a dilemma for them, especially for my mother. There were no special education classes in those days and no guidance for parents other than their common sense and deep religious faith. Dad never gave up on his belief that one day God would cure my vision. The trip did worlds of good for my self-confidence because I encountered no significant problems.

Both my grandmother Carnell and my grandfather Gossett died during my freshman year in high school. Both of these wonderful people played an important role in my life. Grandma Carnell lived close by, and I saw her several times a week. She was a true Southern lady in every sense of the word. Pop Gossett never had any real money, but he had the heartiest laugh of anyone, and he was generous to a fault. In contrast, my grandmother Gossett squeezed every penny tight. "I have to," she said, "or Charlie would give it all away." The song "Sunrise" was sung at my grandmother Carnell's funeral, and this hymn has had a lasting impression on me.[2] Over the last fifty years I have come to understand the meaning of the song: we will awaken from our earthly sleep at the sunrise of our eternal life with him.

My family and I were devastated when Grandmother and Pop died. I saw my dad cry for the first time when my grandmother died. The funerals for both grandparents were huge. We had tons of visitors, and the old family stories were told over and over. There was no doubt about where each one would spend eternity. Once again Preacher Gowan said something at my grandmother's funeral that has stuck with me, "The ones who care the least, cry the loudest."

No teenager ever enjoyed his or her senior class trip more than I did our trip to Washington, DC, on a chartered bus. One of our destinations was the Washington Cathedral, which I had never even heard of, and even though it was still under construction, it dwarfed anything I had ever seen. That trip was an eye opener for so many reasons. We attended a pre-Broadway play. During intermission, a woman sitting in the row behind us heard our southern accents and began to chastise us. "How can you people in the South be so fooled by Franklin Roosevelt? He was nothing but a communist." This was totally unexpected and unbelievable. No one in our experience would ever attack someone in public, and everyone we knew thought that Roosevelt was the savior of the country. My parents, relatives, and everyone we knew spoke of FDR as if he were a member of the family or perhaps even the heavenly trinity.

---

2. Hall, *Songs of faith and triumph*, 5.

We visited all of the usual tourists' sights, including a night tour of the monuments. I still love going to Washington. It is a special place for me. Again, Mother and Dad allowed me to go on this trip. Much of my freedom had to do with their confidence in our leaders. Teachers were held in high esteem. They trusted me, and they trusted Mr. Brissie and Miss Bridges, our chaperones. They listened patiently while I told them every detail of this trip. By now I had already traveled further from home than either of them ever would.

In elementary school, I decided on a course that would guide my life. It evolved slowly and imperceptibly at first, but I can remember when it took root. Dad and I were in some official office in Spartanburg. I am sure we were there about my vision. As we were leaving, I heard a woman say,"I am not going to do that. I will just let the state support me." I can still hear that loud, defiant voice. I turned to my dad and said, "That will never be me."

By example, Mother, Dad, and all of the adults in my world taught me that all honest work is honorable. I did not know the impact of that event at the time, and I have wracked my brain to recover the circumstances, but I knew that from that moment forward, I would never use my poor eyesight as an excuse for not doing what I wanted or needed to do. I was horrified on my visit to the South Carolina School for the Deaf and Blind, where I went to be evaluated for admission at my first grade teacher's insistence. The sight of all those people spending their days making ceramic ashtrays and potholders chilled me to my core. This experience cemented some sort of determination in my soul. Others often tried to persuade me that I should not attempt certain adventures, but lack of visual acuity would never be my excuse. Thanks be to God that I was rejected by the school. I did have to eat my words in biology class at Mars Hill College because all I could see in the microscope was my own eyelash. I am fairly certain that's what I was seeing.

3

Off to College

ALTHOUGH MY FAMILY HAD precious little money and my eyesight was, and still is, terrible, there was never any doubt that I would attend college. Whether I would go was never discussed, at least not in my presence. I'm sure Mother and Dad agonized over it when they were alone. No one had the slightest idea how I would manage or where the money would come from, but my parents had such strong faith that God would make a way. They knew that I had no future at all without a good education. I could never work in the cotton mill. They worried about how I would manage if they weren't around.

It was torment for them to let me go away from home. Mother cried and cried, but she never let me see her tears.

My world grew by leaps and bounds at Mars Hill College, a small Baptist school, located deep in the mountains near Asheville, North Carolina. It was my first extended time away from home. We could not go home nor have visitors for the first five weeks. This gave us a chance to become acclimated to our new surroundings and to begin to exercise control over our lives without the presence of our parents. I was exposed to students and faculty from other parts of the United States and, indeed, from other countries. I became friends with a student from the Cherokee Indian Village and a girl from Cuba, a friendship I seriously impaired when I announced that Cuba was an American territory. I had a lot to learn.

Mars Hill, a junior college at the time, was the right place for me. I was far from home, away from any protective eyes, and I not only survived, I thrived. This became the pattern for my life. Time after time, I put myself in circumstances where I knew no one and had to make it without a protective helping hand. My motto became, "I fly by faith." Although it sounds trite or contrived, it is true. I made friends, never wanted for a date, became a member of the debating team, was on the newspaper staff, and became president of the most prestigious literary society on campus. For the first time, I was on an equal footing with the other guys because no one was permitted to have a car. None of those cute girls had to know that I could not see well enough to drive. I did not have to double date as I did in high school. I became Mitch instead of Mitchell, except to my mother and close family.

The first few months weren't easy. I couldn't see the writing on the chalkboard even from the front row. It wasn't easy talking to the professors about this and even harder to get up from my seat and walk up front to look at the board. Mr. Howell, my math professor, would ask out loud, "Mr. Carnell, it doesn't embarrass you to walk up to the board, does it?" Of course it embarrassed me. I died a little every time he uttered those words. There was the cutest red-headed girl sitting next to me that I wanted desperately to impress, but it never happened. I never worked up the courage to even ask her for a date. When it came to my self-confidence, Professor Howell's words were killers.

During my first semester, I signed up for twenty-one hours of credit, including Spanish. Everyone told me that was the easiest foreign language to learn. Our Spanish professor was a brand new PhD and spoke with an accent. I am certain she was an excellent teacher; however, I flunked Spanish. I had always been a good student and flunking a course was devastating. It caused my parents anguish and great financial hardship. They had not planned on the extra expense of summer school. I did get a head start on French and enjoyed a wonderful summer romance, but I learned a great lesson too late. Don't date your French tutor. It's great fun but not good for the grade point average. I remember a lot more about her than I do about French grammar. I was heartbroken when she did not return for the fall semester.

Off to College

I didn't have a Bible with print large enough that I could study for my Bible class. All those years in Sunday school really paid off. When my spirits were at their lowest, I received a book in the mail from my high school speech teacher and school superintendent, Mr. Brissie. It was great to get the book, *The Art of Seeing*, but it was the words of encouragement in his inscription that lifted my spirits. Once again he expressed his faith in my ability to overcome the odds. He was responsible for my being at Mars Hill in the first place. He telephoned Dr. Blackwell, president of the college, and told him that I was a bright young man with no money who deserved a college education. "Send him here and I'll see that he gets some scholarship aid," came the reply. Mr. Brissie came to visit me, not only at Mars Hill, but also years later when I was at Louisiana State University in Baton Rouge as well. He was a support at all the crucial points in my life. If anyone ever doubts the influence of Christian teachers, he or she should look at the life of Sam Brissie. He not only included me, but often provided the nudge I needed. He cheered my successes and encouraged me when things did not turn out so well. Once, he invited me to teach his large men's Bible class at First Baptist Church in Woodruff.

As supportive as Sam Brissie was, he also betrayed my great respect for him. In 1983, he published a book about his battles over racial segregation in the school systems of Spartanburg County, *One Man in His Time*. He had an enlightened viewpoint for his time and place, which got him into much hot water. He told me about the book and that he had mentioned me and many of my friends in it. I was anxious to read it, but I was disappointed that he had not sought a mainstream publisher. I was humiliated to read, "Mitchell Carnell, an albino with limited vision, majored in speech at Furman, won a fellowship for his Master's in corrective speech, and is now a doctor of philosophy directing a speech and hearing clinic."[1] Of all the things he might have said, this was a total reversal of what I imagined he might say. He chose to single out a physical characteristic over which I had no control. I had tried so hard to be just a regular student. This citation showed me

---

1. Brissie, *One Man in His Time*, 99.

just how badly I had failed. This man, who had fought so hard for racial desegregation, had no sensitivity to physical disabilities. Now I was thrilled that he had not sought a mainline publisher and only a few people would have access to the book. I knew that it would not be reviewed by any significant newspaper or journal. I never told him of the hurt or disappointment; however, when he asked me to ghost write the story of his life, I declined, directing him to another former student of his, Joe Gentry, a very successful school superintendent in Rock Hill, South Carolina. We continued to have a good relationship, but it was never again the same for me. I prayed fervently to be able to forgive him. It took a long time and lots of prayer because the disillusionment was so great.

Because seeing was such a pervasive problem for me, I thought my poor eyesight was the biggest topic of conversation on campus. Imagine my surprise when I learned that no one but me ever thought about it. A group of us were horsing around one afternoon, and I broke my eyeglass frames. Jim Grant agreed to drive me to Ashville to get new frames. We got a ticket for speeding in Weaverville. The judge was Jim's former Sunday school teacher. When I was called to the stand as a witness, the lawyer asked me how fast we were going.

"I think," I started to say before he interrupted me.

"Young man, we don't care what you think. What do you know?"

When I returned to campus with a different pair of eyeglass frames, several people commented.

"Mitch, I didn't know that you wore glasses."

What a revelation! I thought everyone knew. I thought everyone discussed my poor eyesight at every opportunity.

Alcohol in any form was absolutely forbidden in my dad's house, although he drank in his bachelor years. Uncle Jack drank, and my Aunt Alice's husband—their marriage became public after his death—was a fall-down drunk. Beer was not only forbidden but was also considered low class. Alcohol was also forbidden on the campus at Mars Hill. Through my friendships, I learned that a lot of Christians kept beer in their refrigerators at home and drank it. This was foreign to my beliefs. I had a hard time reconciling the notion that Christians could drink alcohol. This discovery was far more dramatic and disturbing than the telling of it can portray. People who drank in Woodruff kept it hidden or were the subjects of gossip. People often parked their cars in front of the liquor store on Main Street on Saturday afternoon to watch who went in and out. It would be several more years before I would actually see nuns drinking beer and wine. Later I saw ministers of other faiths drinking. Imagine my shock the first time I saw Baptist ministers consuming alcohol. I had a lot to learn, and this was perhaps one of the easiest lessons of all, but not at the time. It was traumatic.

It was also at Mars Hill that I first became aware that ministers could be far from perfect in the examples they set. One Sunday, our pastor announced that some members of the Billy Graham Crusade would be on campus the following week. Then he said, "If we meet you and I say, "Hello, Sue," and your name is Mary, then you just pretend that your name is Sue. We want them to know what a friendly campus we have here."

I had never heard a minister encourage someone to lie. I was horrified. Sure, I know that I over-reacted, but I was (am) an idealist.

After that example I heard him make many historical errors in his sermons. He essentially lost his effectiveness as far as I was concerned. He had lost my trust. At that point I would have made a good—no, a great—Pharisee. I was not challenged by his sermons, but that's because church was much more of a social event. Church attendance was required in those days, and you wanted to be with your friends anyway. Bible classes were pleasant but more like an extended Sunday school; therefore, I did not have the trauma of faith many teenagers have when they go away to school. Dorm discussions were much more about girls than religion.

During my first year at Mars Hill, I wanted to interview the black principal of the all-black high school in Woodruff for a paper I was writing. Of course, Dad drove me to see him. I asked him many questions, which he answered easily and graciously. After the interview, Dad was very unhappy with me. I had constantly called the principal "mister," which I had always been taught was proper for referring to an older male. "What should I have called him?" I asked.

"Either professor or uncle," He answered coolly.

"I can't call him mister, but I can make him a member of our family? This doesn't make any sense," I complained.

There was no response, only a silent ride home. The incident was never discussed again.

During those years, there was a black woman, Deanie, who took care of our family's washing and ironing. We took the laundry to her early in the week and retrieved it at the end of the week. This had gone on for years. My parents were very fond of Deanie. Dad had to go into many homes to deliver a range or refrigerator or sometimes to repossess one. He often was stunned at "how nasty" some of these appliances were in white homes. "I had rather eat off Deanie's kitchen floor than on some of their tables." He would exclaim. "Her house is clean."

Before I was school age, we often visited "Aunt Matt" on a Sunday afternoon. She lived in a shack out in the country. Matt, a black woman, had been a young girl during the last days of slavery. There was a bond between her and my mother. According to my Aunt Lala, Mother and her two brothers Jim and Clayte loved Aunt Matt. In fact, when they were very young children, Matt stayed with them on those weekends when my grandparents were away. The three of them would fight to be the ones to sleep next to her.

The last time we visited her before her death, she had picked a pan of blackberries for my mother. No one ever told her that the berries were spoiled. She died soon after. What does one do with all of these mixed messages of love, inclusion, and separation? It takes a lifetime to sort them out. Perhaps it takes an awakening such as I experienced at St. Paul's. There was a connection, a warmth, between black and white people, especially those we knew personally, that defies explanation; but there was also a disquieting separation. I am thankful that Mother and Dad never taught us to hate, but they were prisoners of their time and place. Somehow they prepared our hearts for what was to come in race relations in the South. They sensed the world was changing.

Off to College

Rev. J. L. McCluney, who had become pastor of my home church in Woodruff, came to visit me at Mars Hill. In a discussion with a group of my friends in the snack shop, he said perhaps the most important thing I ever heard him say. "Mitch, everyone is either a missionary or a mission field." At the time, I thought he was being clever with a bunch of college kids and playing for laughs. Now I realize what a profound truth he was stating. His statement became a touchstone for my life.

There were many preacher boys at Mars Hill with whom I became friends. Paul Stouffer from Chambersburg, Pennsylvania, invited me to go and critique his sermon when he preached in a small mountain church. This led to many wonderful discussions. Paul served as a missionary to Brazil after graduating from seminary. Mom and Dad were very fond of Paul. They liked Mars Hill, and especially my friends there.

Dr. Hoyt Blackwell, president of Mars Hill, was scheduled to speak in Woodruff, and my parents felt obligated to invite him to have Sunday dinner at our house. This was major. My dad did not graduate high school. Our house was very modest to say the least. Mother worried herself almost crazy. "How will we talk to this educated man? What will he think of us? What will we serve?" The big day came. Dr. Blackwell was as easy to talk with as our next-door neighbor. He put my parents at ease and was graciousness personified. He and my dad walked in the front yard, talking like long-lost friends. After he left, Mother cried and cried. The tension was finally over. "He's just like one of us," she sobbed. This wonderful man was accustomed to meeting people from all walks of life. He recognized and affirmed by his attitude that my parents were the salt of the earth. His example taught me that one can be at home in any situation, if he knows who he is and is comfortable with himself. Dr. Blackwell gave my entire family a gift that day, worth far more than he could have possibly realized.

Without a doubt, Raymond DeShazo influenced my life more than any other person at Mars Hill. Papa De, as he was called, taught English and speech. He was a stickler for correct grammar and the first choice pronunciation of words. He was the toughest grader I encountered in my entire college career, but he contributed far more than a love of correct punctuation. At the beginning of each class, he read a thought for the day, gleaned from great writers and thinkers. We were expected to write them down. I still have my copies and have read and reread them many times. "Whom the gods would destroy, they first make angry." "The mills of the gods grind exceedingly slow, but exceedingly fine." "Sir, these paintings are not on trial." He pushed us to think and to be creative. He was the right combination of disciplinarian, encourager, and taskmaster.

Mrs. DeShazo was a beauty and a charmer. One day she said to me, "Papa De says that you are getting to be quite a creative writer, but you need to learn to spell." This is a moment that I treasure. It is validation from a highly prized source.

Our debate team was a close-knit group. We made many trips to other colleges to participate in local and regional events. We enjoyed a number of successes as well as a few defeats. Our coach, Dr. Harley Jolley, set very high standards for his students, but he was an extremely nice guy. Joe Chris Robertson, an art professor, often traveled with us. His sense of humor helped on those long trips home when we hadn't done so well. I took an art class with him, and a couple of days into the course he said, "I received permission to use nude models this year, but Mitch Carnell enrolled and wanted to use Braille." He also gave me a great gift. He was interested in my perspective on any given art project. He wanted to know how I saw things. He taught me that my perspective might be different, but it was no less valuable. He encouraged me and let me know that my vision was no barrier for the creative process.

It was on one of these debate trips to Furman University that I first met Joan Lipscomb Solomon. Our paths would cross again many years later and far from Furman. My success on the debate team helped pave my transition to Furman and earned me a small assistantship to work with the debate team.

I left Mars Hill in June of 1954 a far different person than when I arrived in the fall of 1952. I was much more independent, confident, and self-reliant. Yet, Mars Hill College was a sheltered environment that carefully controlled our glimpses of the real world. Contacts between the sexes were carefully supervised. Dialogue in even classic dramas was altered so as not to inflame passions or assault delicate ears. Nude pictures on the covers of art magazines were torn off before the offending publications were placed in circulation. Joe Chris Robertson, my art instructor, was highly incensed by this practice. "Don't they realize that the partially clad body is far more provocative than a totally nude one?"

There was never anything even slightly controversial in the student newspaper. This approach seemed strange, since the founders of Mars Hill took great pride in having chosen the school's name in reference to Paul's sermon at Mars Hill. In that sermon, Paul publicly and forcefully challenged the religious thinking and practices of the day.

What Mars Hill offered was a caring community composed of committed Christians—a collage of fellow students and faculty seeking to serve their faith while searching for deeper meanings and elusive truths. What a great atmosphere! It allowed us to grow in every way in which we were capable of growing. Northside Baptist Church and my family prepared me well to experience this exceptional community.

If Mars Hill sought to protect its students from the harsh realities of the real world, Furman University sought to prepare students for them. Many of the Mars Hill safeguards were gone. At Furman there were very few restrictions for male students and far fewer ones for females than those at Mars Hill. However, some of the same safeguards were also in place at Furman. Alcoholic beverages and dancing on campus were outlawed. The men's campus and the woman's college or "zoo" as it was called in those pre-feminist, pre-political-correctness days were separated by downtown Greenville, but there were classes for both sexes on both campuses. Students rode university buses, drove cars, or walked to get to the other campus. There was also a large day student population. In addition, the atmosphere was one of a senior college rather than a junior college. Mars Hill seemed to have an easy relationship with the North Carolina Baptist Convention, whereas, Furman was always in trouble with the much more conservative South Carolina Baptist Convention.

At Furman I became friends with a student from Calcutta, India, Gurmit Brasich. Our rooms were adjacent but separated by a thin wall. He sat on my bed while I practiced my speeches for Sara Lowrey's class. He said, "This helps me with my English." What I gained from him was even more important. He told me about his country's traditions and about his religion. I hope I was as good a spokesman for Christianity as he was for his faith.

During my Furman days, I learned a very difficult truth. I was a member of the Student Volunteers, a student group that traveled to small town and rural churches on the weekends and took charge of the morning church services on Sunday. We stayed in the home of the local pastor or those of church members. It was these experiences that opened my eyes to the truth that many of the pastors of these churches were no more ready for integration of the races—and sometimes less so—than their church members. They were doing nothing to lead their flocks to a better understanding of the issues. They were paralyzed by fear. Of course, in Baptist churches, the pastor is hired and fired by the local congregation. There is no bishop or governing body, such as a presbytery, to intervene or offer insulation to soften the blow. Nevertheless, I was still an idealist and felt that pastors should lead. "If the church doesn't lead, who will?" I often asked.

Years later I learned an amazing story from my boyhood friend, Ansel McGill. At the time his story took place, he was studying to be a minister in Southern Baptist churches. After a discussion with his dad on racial relations, his father said, "I hope God calls you to preach only in northern churches." By southern standards, Ansel held radical views on racial equality, but he never wavered from his convictions. One year he left a meeting at the Southern Baptist Convention held in Atlantic City to go hear an address by Dr. Martin Luther King Jr.—not a smart move in the eyes of many southerners during the early days of the civil rights movement. He also marched in some of the protests in North Carolina. When admonished by a church member and told that he could lose his job, Ansel replied, "I may be fired, but I will still have my freedom."

At Furman I fell hopelessly in love with another speech major. She embodied everything I had ever dreamed of: she was attractive, ambitious, intelligent, popular, a terrific conversationalist, had a great sense of humor, and was a thinking Christian. My dad even allowed her to drive his car. This was the ultimate in compliments. Although it seemed to me that we were the perfect couple, our relationship didn't last. I was devastated, for I was certain that we were meant for each other. We had intensive discussions about our future lives. During one of these she said, "Mitch, you will never have any money. If you do have any, you will give it all away." She sensed something about me that I had never questioned. I can truthfully say that money, at that point, had not been a part of my thinking about the future. Her pronouncement caught me off guard. She was more perceptive than I had realized.

She gave me a copy of the little devotional book, *As a Man Thinketh,* by James Allen.[2] Other than the Bible, this book has been the most influential one in my life, not just because it was a gift from her, but also because it packs a tremendous message in a few pages. Like Allen, I believe that we can control our thoughts and attitudes and, thus, take charge of our lives. I am grateful for the many things she contributed to my life, especially the insights I gained from our far-reaching discussions about almost every conceivable topic. Since she was a day student when we met, I was in her home constantly. Her parents were wonderful, gracious people, and the four of us went on many day trips together. I received a large measure of guidance from them, especially her mother. It certainly boosted my ego to date such an attractive, talented girl and to be accepted by such a warm family. Her parents were almost a second set of parents. I felt at ease and at home with them. Her parents attended a very conservative church; however, I only attended a few social events with her. It was evident that she and I were out of step with the thinking of the other young people, who were either not in college or were students at the fundamentalist

---

2. Allen, *As a Man Thinketh,* 15.

Bob Jones University located across town, and light-years away in thinking, compared to Furman. I got along well with them and managed to keep the conversations away from explosive topics, but she was determined to win them over. Her perspective was so much broader than theirs, and she was so much more articulate. She always left with her feelings hurt. They clearly did not accept her, and she resented my not challenging their viewpoint. It was my first real encounter with Christians who had such a narrow viewpoint, but I didn't think that I should try to change them. I had already accepted the doctrine that a person's faith was between him or her and God. In Baptist circles this is spoken of as the "Priesthood of all Believers."

Furman University had a profound influence on my life. Classes were rigorous and discussions challenging. I attended Earle Street Baptist Church where Dr. C. Earl Cooper was the minister. His sermons were works of art. I learned that he spent five hours per day in sermon preparation. It showed. One of his sermons, "Straining at a Gnat and Swallowing a Camel," has stuck with me and often causes me to reexamine a position. In the sermon he told of a father who shot and killed his teenaged daughter because she had worn short shorts in public. We fail to grasp the major reality because we trip over an inconsequential issue. We take something that is marginal and make it central.

Dr. Cooper had gained some fame for his tactics with official letters he received from agencies of the Southern Baptist Convention. When these letters contained spelling, grammar, or punctuation errors, he would circle the errors and return the letters to their senders. "You are representing God. You should not do it carelessly." This went right along with his sermon dealing with, "Once You Set Your Hand to the Plow, Don't Look Back." His sermons were provocative and challenging—far different from those at Mars Hill. During the same time several of us listened regularly to Dr. Roy McClain from First Baptist Church in Atlanta and the host of the radio program, *Baptist Hour*. Cooper and McClain and the discussions their sermons prompted rekindled my enthusiasm for religious inquiry. Dr. Cooper was just the influence I needed.

Off to College

I developed great and lasting friendships at Furman. My roommate, Marvin Cann, had a calming, stabilizing effect on me. He was, and is, an excellent student, a thorough researcher, a penetrating thinker, and a sensitive, committed Christian. In those days he was a ministerial student. Today he is a history professor and noted scholar. Marvin was the roommate and friend I needed. We have remained close, even after all these years. When we get together, it's as if we were never apart. Marvin is both my mentor and friend. Kathy, his wife, is the perfect complement to his disposition. It is rare when a wife melds right into a friendship just as if she were always a part of it. Kathy grew up in Greer, a few miles from Woodruff, and has done so much research on the textile mills of Spartanburg County that I am sure she knows everything about the way I grew up. When Kathy, Marvin, Carol, and I are together, it leads to non-stop conversation. God has to be in a friendship that has not only lasted but has also grown richer and richer for fifty years.

If Marvin is steady and calming, my friend, Bob Kirby, was just the opposite. I never knew what to expect from him, but he was good to the core. It was exhilarating to be around him. We had long walks, even longer talks, and miniature golf games. He was absolutely head over heels in love with his future wife. The two of them became home missionaries out West after seminary.

I also became friends with Bill Bagwell, a member of the public relations staff at Furman. He was such a kind, gentle soul. He is a Quaker, and we have resumed contact after many years. He put into practice what he believed and was often a comforting influence when I was agitated about some great, earth-shaking matter.

Dr. Jack Porter was only at Furman for one year. He did not have his PhD degree when he was my instructor in the speech department. He was in charge of the debate program and technical direction of the university theater. He was responsible for my getting a job at the summer outdoor drama, *Chucky Jack*. Our paths would cross again after forty-two years had passed. It is great to renew old ties and to discover that a bond is still there. One incident which is still fresh in my mind involved the debate team. We met at the Porters' house before leaving on our trip to a tournament at Appalachian

State University. Jack and Mrs. Porter served us chili for breakfast to sustain us on our trip into the North Carolina Mountains.

I was stretched in every way by my experiences at Furman. The inspiring and dedicated lives of the faculty, who shared far more than academic knowledge; the emphasis on rigorous scholarship, no matter where it led; and the devotion to ethical conduct all left their mark. However, nothing surpasses the lifelong friendships that were formed at such a crucial time in my life.

4

Beyond the Ivied Walls

AFTER GRADUATION FROM FURMAN in 1956, my eyes were opened to a whole new aspect of human nature that I had never encountered directly. I was totally unprepared for most of these revelations and lessons, but they prepared me for an experience that I would encounter years later. While working in the new outdoor drama, *Chucky Jack*, in Gatlinburg, Tennessee, I encountered male and female homosexuals for the first time. They were dancers and technical crew members from New York City. There were three gay guys on the crew with our supervisor and me. The supervisor, also gay, took an instant dislike for me, just as did I for him; consequently, I got all the dirty work. Before I knew the score on my teammates, I shot my mouth off, expressing my then disdain for "queers." The truth is that I was shocked to my provincial roots. I had heard rumors about a couple of guys at Furman, but they were not in my circle of friends. Lesbians were not even on my radar screen. To be totally candid, there was also some heterosexual behavior that astounded me. I had truly left my safe little world. Again, I survived in an environment for which nothing had prepared me. The little bit I knew, or thought I knew, about gays came from gossip and dehumanizing jokes.

That summer played havoc with my comfort zone. I had planned on an acting job in *The Lost Colony*, but ended up with a job on the tech crew in *Chucky Jack,* which presented a challenge because of my limited vision. I got to know several of the gay actors and actresses in this Kermit Hunter outdoor drama and became friends with some of them, although I was never totally comfortable. I was so ignorant about them. I began to get an inkling of what their lives were like, but I was too unnerved to get close. I met professional actors from all over the country. I was well received by most of them, especially after it became known that I was on my way to the University of Alabama to pursue a master's degree. They respected me because many of them were interested in higher education, and they saw me as more than just a tech crew member. Liz, my future wife, was in charge of props. We found each other at the staff parties because we were usually the only two sober ones there. Those parties were wild, and we found a safe haven in each other. At the dress rehearsal party, the leading lady was so drunk that she fell and broke her arm. Liz and I could talk for hours about anything or absolutely nothing. My poor eyesight or white hair didn't seem to matter to her at all. When the summer ended, she found an advertising job at Miller's Department Store in Knoxville, and I went to Tuscaloosa, Alabama. We were engaged to be married the next summer.

At the University of Alabama, I had an experience that shook me even more than my encounter with gays at *Chucky Jack,* but it taught me a lesson in such a dramatic way that I have not been the same since. I was in downtown Tuscaloosa and needed to get back to the campus for class. I hopped into the first cab I saw. "I'm sorry," the voice in the driver's seat was saying, "I don't carry white folks. You'll have to get out."

"What?" I asked in disbelief of what I just heard.

He repeated, "You will have to get a white cab. I don't carry white folks."

I wasn't angry. I was shocked and humiliated. Stunned, I got out and found a "white cab." Only once before in my young life had I experienced firsthand such blatant discrimination. While doing my practice teaching at Greenville Senior High School in South Carolina, the lead teacher to whom I was assigned told me that with my poor eyesight I could never be a classroom teacher. To make certain that I wouldn't have a chance to prove him wrong, he gave me a "C" in the course. It was a shock because I had gotten along so well with the students. I never had a problem in the classroom. They were great kids. The seasoned teacher who taught next door was incensed by my grade. It didn't hurt that she was my girlfriend's mother. I received an "A" on the National Teacher's Exam and I have taught successfully for forty-five years with nothing but excellent evaluations. The experience taught me first hand how dehumanizing discrimination can be.

Since I was getting a master's degree in communicative disorders and had my traineeship in the speech and hearing clinic, I was immersed with severely handicapped individuals. Somehow I met this new challenge fairly easily and formed deep friendships. I was learning and growing at a rapid rate. There were marvelous instructors in that program, and they changed my life forever. Dr. Ollie Backus taught us to examine everything, especially our own assumptions. She introduced me to the writings of Paul Tillich, Harry Stack Sullivan, Kurt Lewin, and Carl Jung and immersed us in the work of Carl Rogers. These are very unusual readings for a degree in speech pathology, but they have served me well. Ollie herself was a member of Unity Church.

Ollie believed that not being able to drive a car interfered with my self-esteem. One day she told me that Liz and I should buy a car. "I don't have any money." I said.

"I do," she replied.

"That's wonderful for you, but I don't."

"I'll lend you the money," she continued. "You can pay me back with the same interest I would have gotten at the bank."

This is what we did. We bought a 1954 Chevrolet in 1958, which we grew to love. Liz drove us to Moundville State Park on the Black Warrior River on Saturday mornings, and I would drive on the deserted roads. I only did this a couple of times to get it out of my system and to placate my professor. Ollie meant well, but enough was enough.

Imagine the impact of a professor in a major state university loaning money to someone who could not see and had absolutely no collateral. It was a statement of confidence that I can hardly comprehend even now. Is it any wonder that Ollie Backus stands high on the list of those who helped shape my life? I owe much of my willingness to challenge my own assumptions and those of others to this brilliant but down-to-earth professor. She challenged her students to think big, to test limits, and not to accept easy answers. Rather than asking, "What is the matter with you?" she asked, "Who is the matter with you? To whom have you given over control of your life?"

She often said, "You can't accept this position just because I do. You must work through it yourself." She introduced me to possibility thinking. "If money were no problem, what does your dream look like? Visualize it. Now, what part of that dream can you have today?"

Ollie was the most irritating, frustrating, and challenging professor I encountered in my entire educational experience, and she was the most stimulating, insightful, intellectually curious, and driven as well. Whatever she tackled, she did it with passion. I owe her an enormous debt, and she inspired me to try to pass on that passion for learning to my students.

5

Marriage—The Liz Factor

NO ONE CHALLENGED MY provincialism more than my wonderful new wife, Liz. We were married at Fort Sanders Presbyterian Church in Knoxville, Tennessee, by her father during the summer between my two years at the University of Alabama. Her aunt, Kay Wilcox, an ordained Methodist minister and psychologist, gave us a very nice but modest reception. Neither Liz's parents nor mine had any money. My parents bought my wedding suit from Stein's Men's Store, a lower end men's shop, and gave Liz a portable sewing machine as a wedding present. Her parents gave us a $50 check made out in her maiden name. Liz bought our wedding bands using her discount at Miller's Department Store. She also bought me a summer suit. Years later I learned that she had bought us a dinnerware service, but did not have the money to make the payments. She insisted that she did not want a diamond engagement ring. She knew that I would move heaven and earth to buy one for her. She never relented, even when our fortunes improved.

Her parents were missionaries to the Philippines. Her father was native Swiss, and her mother was from Minnesota. Liz was the most accepting person I have ever met. People did not need to change to be her friend. She had traveled all over the world and seemed to have read everything worth reading. She gently and lovingly challenged all of my provincial notions, but I did not give up without a struggle. Once when I asked her if I should write a thank-you note for a kindness she asked, "Why do you think you thought of it?"

She had strong reinforcements in her sister, Joan, and brother-in-law, Joe. We became instant friends the first day we met in the Knoxville bus station, and I have remained close to Joe to this day. Joan died three years ago, and I miss her terribly. She was one of the best friends I ever had. Her death came only eight years after my beloved Liz's and flooded me with a deep sense of loss. Joan was a truly marvelous person with a great sense of humor. She had tenacious courage and fought her cancer with furious determination. She was a Milton scholar and continued to teach her classes at Marshall University almost to the end. She, too, suffered unbelievable discrimination at the hands of her department's administration after her condition became known to them. They wanted to assign only freshman English classes to this brilliant scholar because, "It is easier to find replacements for freshman classes than it is for graduate level classes." She appealed to the human resource department of the university for assistance. She learned that the university was interviewing for her replacement when she met a potential candidate by accident at her national convention. She was very adventurous. One day her mother asked her, "Joan, don't you ever get frightened?"

"Yes, Mother, I do" she replied. "But I do it anyway." Whenever I become unsure of my path or frightened by what lies ahead, I remember Joan's courage. She took me into her confidence concerning her feelings about dying. She said that she needed to talk. I knew that I was being offered a rare opportunity to share in her readying herself for her home-going. It was so hard. It took every ounce of energy I had to just listen, not to interrupt, and not to utter religious platitudes, but these were the conversations I wish that I could have had with Liz when she was dying. Joan was not afraid of dying, and she trusted me with her innermost thoughts. What a blessing she gave to me!

God was not through with me, although I did not realize how he was leading me to open my mind and my heart. I did not see any pattern to all the pieces of my life. All of my experiences were still in their own little individual boxes.

After spending the summer as a full staff member in the Speech and Hearing Center at the University of Alabama and taking an enjoyable trip to New Orleans, I returned to Furman University as a member of the three-person speech faculty. Liz and I spent several weeks in Woodruff with my parents before my job began at Furman.

We had no money, of course. One day my dad came home from work with a package for Liz. It was a new pair of shoes. She was undone by his thoughtfulness and love. She never figured out how he knew her size or what she would like. She never forgot it. Neither have I. It was a beautiful, unguarded moment of caring. It is one of my most treasured memories of my dad. My parents loved Liz. They knew she was the perfect wife for me. Liz often said to me, "Your mother became my mother." She called my dad, "Pop" and returned his love unashamedly. Of course, she was also very clever. Whenever we did not want to follow one of their suggestions, she would say, "You tell them. They have to love you." It was an easy relationship. She and my sister, Jean, became closer than close and "Bunky," Jean's husband, was absolutely devastated when Liz died. Liz made any situation better simply by being there. Our home was truly an oasis of peace for all who came.

At Furman, I agreed to help the black YWCA in Greenville with a training program in parliamentary procedures. I was warmly received. I could hardly believe it. I was only twenty-four years old, and segregation was still the norm in South Carolina. The two other members of the speech department were remarkable people. Sara Lowrey was a nationally recognized authority on the art of interpretive reading, and Dr. Dorothy Richey was a renowned drama teacher. When the debates developed over the integration of the Greenville Concert Association productions, contenders asked hostilely, "Where will we seat them (blacks)?" Sara Lowrey answered, "Between Dorothy and me."

Sara's mother was a most remarkable woman. She went to Blue Mountain College in Mississippi and, as a freshman, married the college president. She received her master's degree when she was 65 and took her first airplane ride at age 100. I took my young children to visit her when she was 103. She was still very much with it. She had to walk around every few minutes because her joints became so stiff otherwise. Sara and her mother were ardent pacifists. Sara was demoted from department chair at Baylor University in Texas because of her political beliefs. She was a tremendous addition to the Furman faculty. Dr. T. Earle Johnson, head of the speech department at the University of Alabama, confided in me that he wanted to hire her at Alabama, but her political beliefs doomed that possibility. She came to visit us in Tuscaloosa, and we had a wonderful time together. She and T. Earle remained close friends. Here was a courageous person who would not sacrifice her beliefs in order to maintain or to secure a prestigious position.

Living in Greenville put us back in close proximity to my parents and to Joan and Joe. Joe was stationed at Fort Jackson in Columbia. It also reunited me with my boyhood friend, Ansel McGill. During the summer I served as acting director of the Greenville Hearing and Speech Center. By the time the board of directors invited me to stay on as executive director, I had already accepted a position at the Wheeling, West Virginia, Society for Crippled Children. It was hard to leave Furman, but the powers that be had decided not to offer any professional degree programs such as speech pathology. Not only that, I was probably the worst technical theater director in the history of the university. I owe Furman a debt that could never be repaid. It solidified my conviction that an institution can be Christian and pursue the highest academic standards at the same time. God deserves our very best. The faculty and administration demanded and inspired our best efforts, and they were people of remarkable integrity. Dr. Richey resisted pressure to produce what were called religious plays. She insisted that all great drama is religious drama because it carries universal truth. I was a messenger to the South Carolina Baptist Convention in 1992 and voted to sever the historic connection between Furman and the Baptists of South Carolina. It was the saddest of acts for me because I believe the convention desperately needed the influence

Marriage — The Liz Factor

of Furman far more than Furman needed the convention's money. Academic freedom was the issue, and that could not be bargained away for a few pieces of silver. History has proved the wisdom of that dissolution because the South Carolina Baptist Convention has become more and more hostile to rigorous Christian scholarship. Sadly, the remaining Baptist colleges in the state fall woefully short of the academic standards of Furman. Furman has continued its rise as a nationally ranked liberal arts college.

That summer at the Hearing and Speech Center proved to be a snapshot of my future career. I worked with a little boy, and when his mother came to pay the bill, she brought me five silver dollars. I realized that this was all the money she had, but I also knew that her pride would not allow me to refuse the payment. "I know how important these are," I said. "They will be here for you when you are able to redeem them."

A very prominent family made a major contribution to the center in appreciation for the work I did helping their mother regain her speech after a stroke. I not only worked with the mother, but I involved the entire family in her treatment. They were eager to help her and to understand her limitations. All of these marvelous relationships exercised a great hold on Liz and me.

From Greenville we moved to Wheeling, West Virginia, with a U-Haul trailer behind our '58 Chevy. While working at the Society for Crippled Children, I had my first in-depth introduction to Catholics in large numbers. The Society served both the public schools and the parochial schools. We made good friends. There was never a ripple caused by religion.

It was also my first in-depth exposure to poverty in any real sense. Oh, I have known poor families, especially elderly black families. I had grown up in poverty but nothing like this. Steelworkers were on strike, and there were great ghettoes—new to me. Many of the children who came for speech therapy did not have warm winter clothing. I had to change some of my diagnostic procedures because the children did not recognize some of the pictures I used that represented more affluent circumstances.

Our Father

We were members of an American Baptist church, which didn't seem much different from the Southern Baptist churches I had known. The Methodists were the conservative group. The church accepted Liz, a Presbyterian, without question. This was certainly a growth year. Liz and I were the recipients of great acts of kindness from the Kossuth family and from our older neighbors, the Ridells. Our first apartment in Wheeling was in a building owned by George J. Kossuth and his wife. He was an internationally renowned portrait photographer and had his studio and apartment in the Stifel Mansion, which he restored to its original condition. Located on North Main Street, it overlooked the Ohio River. After his heart attack, they had moved to the ground floor. It was the most beautiful apartment I had ever seen. There were large glass walls looking out over an English garden and the river beyond.

On our first night after our long trip over the mountains from Greenville, the Kossuths took us to dinner at Oglebay Lodge, the fanciest place in the city. He gave me a marvelous portrait of Carl Sandburg that he had taken in 1928 when Sandburg spoke in Wheeling. He also offered to teach Liz his method of photographic restoration, but this fell through when we moved closer to my work, away from downtown. We truly hated to leave, for Mr. Kossuth was an inspiration. He had only an eighth grade formal education, but he made himself a force in the music, art, and woodworking communities in addition to having an international following as a photographer. He treated us with respect and caring.

Our new apartment was in a converted school building. It was very nice but lacked all of the grandeur of our previous apartment. It was situated about two thirds of the way up a steep hill. Across the street from the side yard was a creek whose banks were beautifully maintained. When there was snow or ice on the ground, I helped Mr. Ridell push his car up the incline from the street into the garage. Mrs. Ridell rewarded Liz and me with a pot of delicious homemade soup. Our apartment was on the second floor and our kitchen window was practically in the trees. We had a bird feeder on the window ledge beside our kitchen table. I was separated from the birds and squirrels by only a screen in the summer. I was delighted because I could watch these wonderful creatures close-up for the first time.

At the Wheeling Society for Crippled Children, I developed a special project for preteens who were stutterers. The program used social situations for them to practice fluent speech and to build self-esteem. None of the students had ever eaten in a restaurant; therefore, none of them had ordered from a menu. They collected menus from restaurants, and these became our practice materials. They worked hard because I promised to take them as a group to the restaurant of their choice at the end of the program. They would order their own meals. They chose the restaurant at Olgebay Park, which even in those days was fancy. This was an integrated group. Since it was 1960, I called to make a reservation and to check out their policies. I reached someone in the kitchen. When I asked if the restaurant was integrated, the voice on the other end answered," Oh, no. We don't have any of that." Realizing that he had not understood my question, I tried again. "I want to bring a group of young black and white students to lunch. Is that alright?"

"Oh, yes," came the reply. "Just not in bunches."

The lunch was a high water mark for all concerned. Every youngster was able to order his or her lunch. Our waitress was extremely patient and gracious. I had not briefed her. These were all severely disadvantaged students with the added burden of their speech problems. None of them could have afforded to eat there, and without this program could never have dreamed of eating there. It was an experience none of us will ever forget. It stands as one of the highlights of my career. It was by every possible measure an unqualified success. After that day, a whole new world stretched out before these young people. They knew now that they could have a much brighter future than they had ever imagined. I thanked God for this day and for these young people and for allowing me to be a part of it.

We left Wheeling with Liz eight and a half months pregnant for me to pursue my PhD at Louisiana State University and to work at the Cerebral Palsy Center of Baton Rouge as a speech language pathologist. It was a long trip in our un-air-conditioned Chevy in late July. I kept an eye out for the highway patrol in case we had an emergency. We stopped to visit Joan and Joe in Newport, Arkansas to break the trip. They had an air-conditioned apartment. Joe was on the newspaper staff there. The visit was far too short. The two sisters never had enough time together, and Joe and I always had plenty to talk about.

We arrived safely in Baton Rouge, and Suzanne was born on August 23 in the Baptist hospital. Joan was scheduled to come and help Liz, but her daughter, Anne, had gotten sick, so we were left to our own devices. The staff of the Cerebral Palsy Center acted like mother hens and even hosted a baby shower for me. Somehow we survived, and Suzanne thrived.

At Goodwood Baptist Church, my mind got a gentle nudge. Rev. Blackmon had a statue of St. Francis in his study. I had never known a Baptist pastor with a Catholic statue. The church had paid nursery workers dressed in white uniforms, and the women were wonderful with Suzanne when we started taking her to church. I taught a young adult Sunday school class made up of young professionals and graduate students. I am not clear on how that came about, but it was a delightful experience. After the LSU vs. Mississippi football games, it was absolutely futile to try to discuss a Sunday school lesson.

Our closest friends were Catholic, Episcopalian, and professing atheists. One professing atheist couple sent their daughter to a Methodist preschool because,"We don't want her to be ignorant about God and Jesus when she goes to school." One day their daughter came home and reported, "God's home." The minister had returned from his vacation.

The friendships we made in Baton Rouge remain strong. Liz and I did not drink even wine at that time. When we attended a party at the home of our friends, Don and Nan Lewis, Nan met us with a glass of cranberry juice or ginger ale. She is thoughtful, witty, and very attractive. She was the psychologist at the Cerebral Palsy Center, and Don was a psychology professor at LSU. Lois Klink mothered us and is a great friend. June and Tom Smyth helped us keep our sanity. June was a teacher of handicapped children. Tom

Marriage—The Liz Factor

worked for the State personnel system. They had twin daughters a little older than Suzanne and later had a son about the same time we had Mike. They later added another daughter. We spent many happy times together. June made wonderful coffee in a stovetop pot that she dared anyone to clean. Both Tom and June had a zest for living that was radiant. The twins attended Vacation Bible School at Goodwood with Suzanne, and June raved about how many Bible verses they learned in two weeks.

The Cuban Missile Crisis ignited while we were in Baton Rouge, and the city was flooded with Cuban refugees. Somehow I was asked to teach a course in oral English for them at the YWCA. The television program that featured Mitch Miller, *Sing Along with Mitch*, was popular at the time; therefore, my courses quickly became known as "Speak Along with Mitch." What a turn of events. Remember, I flunked Spanish at Mars Hill College. This exposure and acceptance by members of a different culture broadened my knowledge and appreciation for people whose backgrounds were far removed from my own. Again, the teacher learned more than the students.

One night when I came home from class and was still on the sidewalk, I could hear Suzanne's labored breathing although we lived on the second floor. She had croup. We made a tent for her, complete with a cold-steam vaporizer, and I stayed under it with her nearly all night. I was holding her most of the time. Each time she awakened herself with her croaky coughing; she would clutch me tightly and say," I love you, Daddy." She was scared, and so was I. Even today, she never leaves or ends a long distance telephone call without uttering those magic words, "I love you, Daddy." I finally got to the point where I could respond or even say them first. Following this harrowing night from her childhood, she was hospitalized the next morning. Liz and I were petrified, but she made a remarkable recovery.

In the late afternoons I took Suzanne on walks around our neighborhood. Sometimes I pulled her in her little red wagon, or she would ride her tricycle. Most of the time, I ended up carrying both Suzanne and her tricycle. On one of those walks, I picked up a brick from a construction site to put on our garbage can to keep the neighborhood dogs out. I couldn't sleep that night, thinking about what a bad example I had set for my baby girl by stealing a brick. Early the next morning I took it back.

Even though I was a student at LSU, I was also employed to teach two graduate courses dealing with neurological impairments. One of my fellow students and a student in the classes I taught was Susan Shanks. Susan had contracted polio as a teenager and was in a wheelchair. Her mother took her everywhere. I never heard Susan complain about her physical condition. She was the "brain" of our group. After graduation, she became head of the speech and hearing program at Fresno State University in California and has several books to her credit. She is an inspiration.

Liz suffered a miscarriage in 1962. I did not realize until many years later how deeply it affected her. The pregnancy was so new that it was just not real to me, but it left her with deep emotional scars. I can't imagine how insensitive I must have seemed to her. We were thrilled when Michael was born on July 24, 1963, very healthy, with no signs of any difficulty. When I called my parents to announce his arrival and to tell them that his name was Claude Michael, Mother exclaimed, "You kept your father's name!" She called to Dad, "Claude, they named the baby after you." I had no idea that such a simple gesture would bring them so much joy. Moments like that stay with you and warm you forever.

We were in a staff meeting at the Cerebral Palsy Center on November 22, 1963, when we were interrupted with the news that President Kennedy had been shot. Paula Eagle, our director, Sally Coperthwaitte, and I were scheduled to leave the next day for the convention of the Cerebral Palsy Association in Dallas. At first the convention was cancelled, but then it was held as a memorial to the fallen president. What a terrible mistake. There were blaring television sets everywhere and tons of police and secret service agents. Paula was a Kennedy disciple, and she was devastated. We were there in the hotel lobby watching the television when Jack Ruby shot Lee Harvey Oswald. What a nightmare. The place went wild. Paula was in tears most of the time, and she consumed far too much alcohol. It was a traumatic experience for everyone. Not much was accomplished in the scientific sessions. I did have an opportunity to meet many of the important professionals at the meeting, including Dr. Martin Palmer, founder of the Institute of Logopedics in Wichita, Kansas. I could not know then that years later, I would be a finalist in a nationwide search for his successor after his death.

We loved Baton Rouge, and life at LSU was about as good an experience as one can have. I developed an internship program between the speech department and the Cerebral Palsy Center. I had a blossoming private practice, and we had made a place for ourselves in the community. We loved Goodwood Baptist Church, and Suzanne and Mike had playmates. It was a great temptation to stay there, but I was thirty years old with a wife and two children. I was ready to make my mark in the world. Dr. Waldo Braden, head of the speech department and a mentor, urged me to go to the Charleston Speech and Hearing Center for three to five years, and then he would find me a chairmanship of a speech department somewhere. He kept a large map of the United States on the office wall and pins were stuck into it at every place where an LSU graduate was a department head. Having Dr. Braden's blessings was a terrific plus for launching a career. He was my ideal of what a true professional should be. This department was so professional that you did not expect it to be warm and nurturing, and yet you became a member of a very close and supportive, but demanding, family. I did not expect this department to be peopled by committed Christians since it was in one of those big, bad, state institutions, but I learned how wrong stereotypes can be. It was very hard to leave, but we were excited by our new challenge.

6

Home at Last

WE KNEW WE WERE home when we arrived in Charleston, South Carolina, late on August 21, 1964. What a warm, beautiful, gentle, historic city—everything the travel guides say it is and much, much more. People are gracious and kind. The board of directors at the Speech and Hearing Center where I would serve as executive director were mostly from Charleston society, but they defied the old stereotypes of being uppity and unfriendly.

DeRossett Myers, a prominent lawyer, had the soul of a gentleman. He was as liberal in his politics and religion as anyone I had ever met. Dewar Holmes was the image of a southern dowager, but a warmer, more dedicated person never existed. She could cut to the heart of an issue in nothing flat. She simply called things as they were. She and Baron, her husband, adopted us. Vereen Coen was the dynamo that kept things humming. Her mother was the founding president of the organization. Tilly Mosley was a jewel with a quick wit and a slashing tongue. O. Johnson Small was the financial wizard and the rock of Gibraltar. Tom Careere was an educator's educator. If there were a way to help children, he would find it. Lester Hamilton knew everybody. He lived in North Charleston, which at the time was frowned on by the folks in Below Broad Charleston, but Lester was liked and respected by everyone. He became my close friend. I was only 30. These wonderful people took me under their protective wings. I loved them, and I think it safe to say that they loved me.

They loved me when I spoke in Mt. Pleasant, across the Cooper River from Charleston, about mentally retarded children and the natives were incensed—they did not view the children there as handicapped. They loved me when Tom Careere and I started a racially integrated public school program for hearing impaired children, even though mixing races wasn't socially accepted in the South in 1966-67. That board taught me something. When I interviewed for the executive director's position and they asked me to spell out my vision for the future, I stated, "If you are looking for someone who will operate a segregated center, you need to look for someone else."

Their answer astounded me. "Neither would we operate a segregated center," they said. They were interested in helping children learn to talk and hear—all children. They never retreated. They already understood far better than I what "Our Father" really meant. This board had a quality that is extremely rare in any organization. It was more than civic duty to them. They were in love with the mission. I sensed that devotion on my first visit with them, and it remained with me throughout my entire tenure.

There was tremendous camaraderie among the directors of other speech and hearing centers in the state. Tom Walpool in Greenville, Bill Goldman in Columbia and later Anderson, Pat Vincent in Florence, and Dr. Harold Powell, head of the Speech and Hearing Program at South Carolina State College, an all-black institution at that time, were not only friendly toward each other, but they also had a genuine interest to see each other succeed. We integrated a restaurant successfully and peacefully in Aiken, South Carolina, during one of our state speech and hearing association conventions. The atmosphere was extremely tense, but quiet, as we walked through one dining room to the next at the height of the lunch hour. I integrated the staff at the center and served as PTA president the first year Suzanne's elementary school was integrated. Parents and teachers believed that I possessed the skills and self-control to make a smooth transition to new concepts in thinking.

The first time we had an integrated PTA board meeting, it was at our house. The white members arrived first. We had just purchased a cotton candy machine to use in our fundraisers. Liz and I set it up in the hall bathroom where there were tile walls, and everyone was gathered there to see the machine operate. When the black member arrived, I answered the doorbell and said, "We are all in the bathroom. Come on in." We had a trouble-free year.

We entertained black staff members as well as black friends of Suzanne and Michael in our home. Everyone knew that our home was a safe place to be. I had some wonderful black staff members who made it easy—Vivian Pickney, Markeitha Green, and later, Deloris Simmons. Mamie Blidgen was amazing with the children of the center, but Mamie was of the old school. She would work with us, but she would not socialize with us. Mamie taught little boys to use the toilet by having them urinate in a tin can so they could hear the loud sound it made. She was an absolute delight.

I invited one of the white volunteers at the Speech and Hearing Center who had also been a foreign missionary to have dinner at our home. This sweet, generous lady had given her entire social security check one month to buy a hearing aid for a young black boy. "Mr. Carnell," she said matter-of-factly, "My husband won't eat with you."

"Why not? I don't even know him."

"Because you socialize with black people," she said.

She invited Liz and me to her home for lunch when her husband was out of town. I never understood how such a wonderful woman could be married to a man with such a different value system.

The South Carolina Speech and Hearing Association had never had a paid outside speaker. I arranged with the Cerebral Palsy Association to co-sponsor Dr. Boyd Sheets, head of the program at Brooklyn College. He was such a wonderful person and was my first real interaction with a Mormon. He was graciousness itself. During that same meeting I had learned that Richard Nixon would be at a meeting in the same hotel. Nixon was chairman of the President's Committee on Employment of the Handicapped when he was vice-president.

I asked General Mark Clark, president of the Citadel and his host for the meeting related to mutual fund companies, to invite Nixon to speak to our little group. When I telephoned the General to follow-up on Nixon's response, Mrs. Clark informed me that the General would not do it. "If you want Mr. Nixon, you will have to invite him yourself," she advised. When I called the Francis Marion Hotel, I was dumbfounded when the operator gave me Nixon's room number. I was even more amazed when he answered his own telephone. Not only did he talk with me, but he agreed to speak to our group. The next morning the news crews caught sight of him coming down the hall to our meeting and followed him. Instead of just a word of greeting, we got about a fifteen-minute speech. I talked with him afterwards, and he seemed genuinely pleased to be there. He informed me that his sister's child had gone to the John Tracy Clinic in California.

Dr. Sheets did not let a teaching opportunity pass. To emphasize the importance of interpersonal relationships in the therapeutic relationship, he told us how, at that moment, we felt very warmly toward Mr. Nixon and even warmer toward the Republican Party because Nixon has established a personal connection with us. Dr. Sheets was so impressed with our group that he offered to return his honorarium. Dr. Sheets changed my impressions of Mormons. I was impressed by the way he conducted himself. Even at cocktail parties and other social events, he was very comfortable with who he was. It was a real learning experience for me. He lived his values without making others uncomfortable. He set a high standard for all those speakers who would come later. He was exactly the right choice. He understood the *our* in "Our Father" far better than I did at the time.

7

Hard Lessons

IT WAS SATURDAY NIGHT, 1986, and Dad was in the hospital. I was in Woodruff to take care of Mother, who was suffering with Alzheimer's disease. I left the hospital not expecting him to live through the night because he was so weak. He was too weak for gallbladder surgery. For the first time in my life, I literally prayed through the night that God would spare his life. He looked so helpless and fragile, and he was so worried about Mother that he could not rest. Even in his condition, she was his major concern. It was a long, sleepless night but morning finally came, and my prayers were answered. Dad was sent home from the hospital to gain strength for surgery, which would come later. God obviously was not ready for him. He would live almost another year, but he never regained his previous vitality.

Dad never had a firm grasp on what I did for a living. From the day I left for college, he felt uncomfortable around my new friends. He thought that I was ashamed of him and his lack of formal education. I suffered from the feeling that he was disappointed in having a son who did not play ball, fish, drive, or have a real job. This was not something that either of us could talk about. Here we were, two grown men—father and son—neither feeling that he measured up to the other's expectations. All of this changed when my book, *Speaking in Church Made Simple*, was published by Broadman Press in 1985. He kept it by his chair. He read it over and over. He showed it to everyone. It was almost as if suddenly all the sacrifices that he and Mother had made to put me through college had paid off. I think the book made up for my not becoming a minister, because he did not show the same enthusiasm about my first book, *Development, Management and Evaluation of the Community Speech and Hearing Center*. He and Mother had always nourished a gnawing fear about what would happen to me if he and she weren't around. He gave me a parcel of land so I would always have a place to live. My marriage to Liz, whom they dearly loved, and this book did away with those fears at long last. For the first time in my life, I knew I had his approval. At least I knew he was no longer ashamed of me. My old defensiveness went away. I finally had my father's blessing. I probably had had it all along, but didn't know it.

I still had another lesson to learn about my dad. When he died unexpectedly, we were met head-on with the problem of what to do about Mother, since she was now in the advanced stages of Alzheimer's. I was totally unprepared for what I heard from my dad's pastor at his funeral. "Many times Mr. Claude has come to me and asked, 'Preacher, please pray for Imogene and Mitchell. They are having a tough time.'"

Dad had never said a word about this to me. It never occurred to me that he was making prayer requests for us, even though I knew that until his death, Liz's father had prayed for us daily by name. I wish I had known because it had been such a good feeling every day knowing that prayers were prayed on our behalf when Dr. Frei was interceding for us. I missed that feeling. It was another indication of how much Dad and I had missed out on with each other because of our stubbornness. "Bull headed" was his term for it. We were both much too private, or perhaps too afraid, to expose our emotions. It would not be manly. One day when Dad said to me in exasperation, "You are the stubbornest white man God ever let live," Mother chimed in, "Well, you know where he got it."

Jean, my sister, drove the ninety miles between Lincolnton, North Carolina, and Woodruff several times a week. She was physically and mentally exhausted. When the hospital telephoned to tell us of Dad's death, both Liz and I were so worried about her that we thought the call was about Jean. Her sacrifices of time, energy, and her own family responsibilities were unbelievable. No one could satisfy Dad's concern for Mother. He wanted his friend back. He wanted—no, he expected—Jean to be there day and night. It was not easy for her, but she continued these trips even after Dad's death to check on Mother. Unfortunately, Jean suffered the brunt of his frustration and felt a deep sense of guilt that she had not done enough. Nothing could be further from the truth. I will never understand how she did all that she did. She was their rock. No one could have possibly done more. Dad knew this, but he never said it to her. What a tragedy. We leave too many things unsaid—too much love goes unspoken. My sister is one of my heroes. She has a greater capacity to love than anybody I know.

Liz and I, mostly Liz, decided to bring Mother to Charleston over Jean's protests. She finally agreed for us to bring Mother just for the summer. Although it disrupted our well-ordered lives, neither of us ever regretted our decision, even for a moment. Mother could do nothing for herself. We did everything for her without exception. We did have help from the home health agency on weekday mornings. Mother never lost her pleasant disposition or her wonderful smile. Her grandson Darrell could always bring a smile to her face, as could young babies. Darrell picked her up and danced with her. The rest of us treated her like fine crystal. I can hardly write this because Mother was such a wonderful, caring, fun-loving person. The disease literally destroyed her before our eyes. It was torture to be a helpless observer as the destruction took place.

She was my rock, my encourager. She had faith in me when there was no reason for it. I was in high school and wanted to take a course for would-be writers through correspondence that cost only $9.95. Dad thought it would be money wasted. "Claude," she said, "If we don't encourage him, who will?"

She did not encourage my learning to drive a car, but Dad taught me anyway. She also said that she would never buy me a knife or a gun, and she was true to her word. Perhaps the best story of my mother's ferrous defense of me happened when I was still very young. I don't remember the incident but it has been recounted to me many times. We went on a Sunday afternoon to get ice cream at Ponder's Ice Cream Shop in Greer, twenty miles away. This was a real special treat. Aunt Alice was with us. "Edith," she said, "You are staring at that woman."

"Well," Mother said. "She is staring at Mitchell."

Mother taught me the principle of paying it forward long before I knew there was a name for it. Just before I went to Mars Hill College, one of my uncles was talking about what his son owed him for his college education. Mother chimed in, "The only thing Mitch owes us is to do the same for his children."

Mother's illness brought out the best in Dad. He had even less patience than do I, but he was so gentle with Mother. He would sit holding her hand for hours and talk to her, even though she understood nothing he said. We had a party for their fiftieth anniversary at Antioch Baptist Church between Woodruff and Enoree. Mother was barely able to be there. Someone said to Dad, "Claude, fifty years is a long time, isn't it?"

His answer startled me. It was so out of character for him, but it captured their relationship perfectly. "Not nearly long enough," came the swift reply. Mother died in her sleep a year and a half after Dad's death. When Dad died, we were not certain at first whether Mother understood what had happened or not, but when we rolled her wheelchair up next to his casket, tears streamed down her cheeks. She knew.

I have never doubted that Dad loved Jean and me, but he had absolutely no understanding of how to express it. He provided for us, protected us, worried about us, encouraged us, called us, came to visit us, and defended us to others, but he could not verbalize feelings other than when he was angry or upset. I remember sitting on his lap as a child, and he would pretend to beard me with his heavy beard. We took short family trips together and for the most part, we had a good life together. On one of those Sunday trips into the North Carolina mountains in the summer of 1941, Dad stopped the car along the side of the road to admire an apple orchard. He and I got out of the car and walked a few feet away. A man came toward us, and Dad told me to get back in the car.

He and Dad talked in hushed tones. When Dad got back in the car, Mother asked, "What did that man want?" "He wants to buy Mitchell. He says boys like him can use a stick to find water." I did not understand this until years later when I saw the movie, *God's Little Acre,* with my parents. The movie introduced the notion that an albino could aid in locating gold to be mined.[1] My sister remembers the event, but no one ever spoke of it to me.

When I was in the eighth grade, a stray dog we named Shep took up with us. One day Dad and I were working on a fence, and he reached toward me to grasp the wire I was holding. Shep, thinking that he intended to harm me, grasped my dad's wrist in his jaws and held it. Dad was startled but very pleased. "That dog can stay," he said. He recounted the story to anyone who would listen.

Mother and Dad were dearly devoted to each other, and anyone who came near could see it. Even in the late stages of her illness, Dad sat and held her hand and talked to her for hours. Even in his weakened condition, he somehow managed to get her out of bed every morning and back in bed every night. He never left her alone after she became sick. He learned to bake pecan pies because we had pecan trees on our place, and he always had one ready for us when we visited. In going through his records, I found a cancelled check he had written to Oral Roberts, seeking healing for Mother. Suddenly the desperation Dad felt for Mother and how helpless he felt sank in. He would have done anything, made any sacrifice to save her. Dad had great faith. He prayed for and believed that God would some day heal my vision. He believed that my nephew would give up drinking alcohol when no one else believed it, and he was right. He and Mother were such a team. It is almost impossible to think of one of them separate from the other.

Not long before we celebrated Dad's eightieth birthday, I had a revelation. I had finished talking with him on the telephone. We had been sparring about politics. I told Liz, "Dad is eighty and he isn't going to change. I'm fifty, and I'm not going to change, but

---

1. *God's Little Acre,* directed by Anthony Mann, (1958; West Germany: Security Pictures, 1958).

from now on, anything he says is right. None of this petty stuff matters one bit. Please help me stick to my resolve."

Dad and I enjoyed many long telephone conversations after that. I made it my goal to try to lift his spirits. Our conversations always ended with him being more upbeat and cheerful than when we began. He had changed. There was a time when his long distance calls were brief and to the point—no longer. We usually talked an hour or more.

I cannot remember ever hearing my dad say, "I love you, son." Even worse, I cannot remember ever saying, "I love you, Dad." Even when he was lying in that hospital bed, I felt deeply the love I had for him, but my lips remained silent. Several times I almost worked up the courage to tell him, but the words never came. Why? I am supposed to be the communication expert. I don't know, but it is a regret that I carry every day. It was a terrible failure. Even at that late date, I was afraid or unwilling to make myself vulnerable. Now I try not to repeat my mistake. I tell my family and friends how much I care for them and what they mean to me. One of the bonds Dad and I shared is that he was elected as a deacon at Northside Baptist Church in Woodruff the same year I was first elected as a deacon at First Baptist in Charleston. That brought him great joy and satisfaction.

Whatever reluctance Dad felt about showing outward affection toward Jean and me disappeared completely with the grandchildren. He idolized his grandchildren and made no secret of it. They returned his love in abundance. Whenever any of them had a problem, they knew they could count on Pop to help. I could hardly believe it the night he left the dinner table to go downtown to buy Danny, the first grandson, a tricycle. Nothing was too good for his grandchildren. When Suzanne and Michael were born, he was ecstatic. Since Suzanne was the first and only granddaughter, she could do no wrong. She returned his affection in full measure. She loved spending time with Pop and Mama. She spent a week or so during the summers helping him in the garden. She could not have made him happier.

8

My Darkest Hours

I AM A VERY active member of First Baptist Church in Charleston, South Carolina, the oldest Baptist church in the South. The congregation and its pastor moved to Charleston from Kittery, Maine in 1696. The people of this church nourished my soul when my beloved Liz died. It is the most wonderful fellowship I have ever known. For the almost two weeks Liz was in a coma and I remained in the hospital to be close to her, I was supplied with meals and visitors to keep me company. Our pastor, Scott Walker, never missed a day in visiting, nor did the minister for senior adults, G. W. Bowling. Liz taught preschool at Westminster Presbyterian Church, and her fellow teachers and the children's parents were just as attentive. I could not have made it through this difficult time without these compassionate, caring people.

One night when there were only a few people around, I told Anne and Gil Pooser, members of my Sunday school class, just how troubled I was. "I don't know what to pray for," I said. "I don't want Liz to die, but I know that if she lives, she will be a vegetable."

Anne said, "Mitch, you don't have to know. God knows what's in your heart. He hears your groanings and knows how to interpret them." Then she quoted Romans 8:26 (King James Version): "The Spirit also helpeth our infirmities for we know not what we should pray for as we ought: but the Spirit itself maketh intercession for us with groanings which cannot be uttered." That conversation and her reassurance have stuck with me from that day until now.

My Darkest Hours

I was with Liz in ICU after midnight on Saturday night, with most of the lights turned really low, when Scott came in. "I didn't want a day to go by without being here," he whispered, "One of our members attempted suicide. I have been with him and his family."

Liz died less than a year after Mother's death. Mother died a year and a half after Dad. I don't know if it was because of Liz's death or the combination of the three deaths so close together, but everything I believed and had been taught were challenged. I was already struggling with the fundamentalist's take-over of the Southern Baptist Convention and how to deal with that. Scott Walker and I spent many hours talking during this period. I gradually just focused on what I knew was truth—God loves me. One day when Scott and I were having lunch together at the Olive Garden, he asked me where I was in the process. I told him that I was back where I had started as a child. "All I am sure of," I said, "is that God loves me, and everything else is just explanation."

"Well, Mitch," he said, "If you have arrived at that conclusion, I think you have it." I have never thought much about my own death. I was only fifty-five at the time, but I knew that I was ready to die. I was certainly in no hurry to cross that line, but I have no fear of death for myself. I had not experienced that peace before. Scott encouraged me to rely more on Suzanne and Mike and not try to shoulder everything myself. They were as devastated as I about their mother's death, perhaps even more. Mike internalized everything, and Suzanne was angry. I was in too much pain to really see their suffering, and I'm not sure how much support I offered them. I am afraid that I failed them miserably. I was going through the motions of living. My work kept me busy, but when I came back to an empty house, only my dog, British, kept me from going crazy. He had to be fed, let in and out, and walked. He was a great listener, although he did drift off to sleep more than a few times. For a long time he wandered about the house searching for any trace of Liz. He knew things were not right.

When I visited my daughter Suzanne in Nashville, everything reminded me of Liz. I didn't want to upset Suzanne, but I couldn't restrain the tears. Neither could she. Mike and I somehow got through all the day-to-day, mundane chores. We were all in such pain. We were a closely-knit family. Since Liz did all the driving, we went everywhere together. The separation was almost unbearable for all of us. Nancy, Mike's wife, and Liz were extremely close. She found it almost too painful to come back to our house. Even before Mike and Nancy were married, Nancy spent so much time at our house that it was no adjustment at all when they married. She was already a member of the family.

One day Mike and I were doing our errands and talking about all of the previous events. I said, speaking of Liz's death and the death of my own parents, "One expects his parents to die." Mike interrupted me and tore my heart out; "No, Dad. A son doesn't expect his mother to die."

Rev. Henry Finch was Scott Walker's predecessor at First Baptist. Henry was every church's dream: a great pulpiteer, a dynamic personality, a born leader, a great organizer, and very ecumenical in his theology. He became an in-demand speaker at churches of other denominations in the city as well as at numerous civic organizations. He relished the formality of First Baptist and steeped himself in its history and traditions.

Nothing could have prepared the congregation for the bombshell that struck out of nowhere. Henry was gay and very active sexually. Rumors were rampant. We were devastated, but the church responded in the most loving way possible. It allowed Henry to retire on disability, continued his salary for a time, directed to his wife, and gave their son free tuition at the church-run day school. Unfortunately, as a congregation we never dealt with our grief, hurt, anger, disappointment, and disillusionment as a community of faith. We went on as if we had not been savagely wounded. We desperately needed help, but we did not get it.

Henry was the best organizer I have ever known. His prayers were exceptional. I never cared much for public prayer, but Henry prayed about things and people that I would never have thought of. His prayers were prayers of thanksgiving. They were uplifting. He changed my opinion of public prayer. His sermons were masterpieces, both in content and delivery. He was at home in the pulpit—a natural.

One day my son, Mike confronted me. "Dad, you liked Henry, didn't you?"

"Yes, son. You know I liked Henry."

"Dad, you loved Henry, didn't you?"

"Yes, son. I loved Henry."

"You will remember that the next time you sound off about gays, won't you?"

"Who made you so damn smart?"

Suddenly I was back in Gatlinburg, Tennessee, with the cast of *Chucky Jack* and all those gay dancers and tech crew members. At least I had a little understanding of the dynamics of the situation. Gradually bits and pieces of my life were coming together. God was leading me step by agonizing step to a better understanding of what "Our Father" really means. The pieces of my life keep coming together.

Things were going great at the church until this bombshell struck. Henry was such a great organizer that operations continued to move smoothly for over a year until our new pastor, Scott Walker, arrived. None of us imagined at that time that the gay issue would become a focal issue in all of the major denominations. At First Baptist we certainly thought it was a local matter and hoped and prayed that no one outside the church would learn of our tragedy or our pain. I have watched other denominations as well as my own struggle with this very complicated and divisive issue. I can truthfully say that I learned so much from going through this. My son Michael was right, I loved Henry. Not only did I love him, but I also admired him. You are lucky if you meet one Henry Finch in your lifetime. Henry later moved to Charlotte, North Carolina, where he did marvelous work with the gay community. He taught a highly successful Sunday school class at Myers Park Baptist Church. I saw him only once after he left Charleston, and that was in the Charlotte airport.

When Liz was in a coma at St. Francis Hospital, there were prayer chains literally around the world: every denomination or religious group in the city, friends and relatives around the country, friends in the Philippines, and relatives and friends in Switzerland. Telephone calls poured in from everywhere—all faiths and races: Catholic, Mormon, Methodist, Presbyterian, Baptist, Reformed, Jewish, black, and white. When I was permitted into the intensive care unit, I told Liz about each and every prayer group. I will never know whether she heard me or not, but I know that the mere recitation of the list—Charlotte, Woodruff, Lincolnton, Nashville, New York, San Francisco, Washington, Huntington, Seattle, Manila, and Zurich—gave me strength. All were praying, "Our Father."

Each time I was allowed in, I also repeated the Twenty Third Psalm to her. It gave me strength. Mike and Suzanne read *Winnie the Pooh* to her, as she had done for them as children, and they played Jimmy Buffet music, which she loved, on the radio. Those were terrible, terrible days!

I went by to see the hospital Chaplin, Father Kelley. "Father Kelley," I said, "We are not Catholics, but don't you dare go by intensive care without saying a prayer for Liz." He assured me that I didn't even need to ask.

Suzanne, Mike, and I made the awful decision to disconnect all of the life-giving equipment, but we asked that it be delayed until after Liz's mother had an opportunity to see her one last time. Mercifully, there was a wonderful nurse from the Philippines on duty who very gently explained everything to Mrs. Frei. Suzanne walked into the intensive care unit only seconds after her mother died. She was devastated.

The hospital allowed me to stay in an empty room so I could be nearby, and Mike and I were in my room. Suzanne had the terrible burden of telling us the dreaded news. I had wanted so desperately to be with her when the end came. Liz and I talked about everything over the years. We were lovers, husband and wife, and most of all, best friends. If we could have talked about this, it would not have been so hard. She was my life. My rock. Mike and Suzanne were never out of her thoughts. The four of us were as close as any family can be. How could we survive? What would we do?

My Darkest Hours

My mother's long illness gave Liz and me plenty of time to talk about what each of us would prefer if it came to the point where either of us needed extreme measures to survive. Both the children and I knew her wishes; otherwise, I am not certain that we could have made the decision to withdraw the life supports; nevertheless, it was an agonizing experience. It did not take me long to have a Living Will drawn up for myself because I want to spare anyone else from having to make such a decision.

At Liz's funeral Dr. Scott Walker said the most amazing and most comforting thing. "When that aneurysm hit Liz, God was the first to cry." I have cherished his statement because that is the kind of compassionate God I want. Her funeral and burial were upbeat and marked by hundreds of expressions of love and gratitude for her life. She touched the lives of so many people and always in a positive way. People were in shock. I am told that when her coma was announced at the mid-week prayer service, Margaret Howell gasped, "No," out loud. Liz was a quiet person, but her gentle, loving, caring manner made her welcome wherever she went. Ellen Shealy, president of the Speech and Hearing Center Board, went home from Liz's funeral and told her three daughters, "Things are going to be different from now on. I could not help but wonder what the minister would be saying, if that were me in that casket."

Later Ellen came to my office and said, "Mitch, I need to drive you home from work every day."

When I protested that I already had arrangements in place, she countered. "Mitch, I didn't say that you needed a ride. I said that I need to drive you."

Soon after Liz's death I received an unexpected request, but one I was eager to accept. Christ Our King Catholic Church asked me, a Baptist, to train their lay readers. Arnold Eaves, minister of education at First Baptist Church, and I had heard Pope John Paul II speak during his visit to Columbia in 1987, and we were both impressed that his sermon would have been appropriate in any church. Of course I was apprehensive about accepting the invitation, but Father James Carter told me that he would guide me. I was amused that there was a Catholic priest named Jimmy Carter.

He was true to his word. We met on two Saturday mornings and had a great time. When I finished the training, he assured me that I had not said or done anything that would not be appropriate in any church. This was truly one of the high moments of my religious life. My insight was growing little by little. God was leading me toward a greater understanding of what it means to be his child—a member of his family. I could never have imagined being asked to assist in training in a Catholic church, but God often surprises us. I wish Liz could have known, but maybe she did. It would have thrilled her.

I made many trips to visit Joan and Joe in Arlington, Texas. During these visits I became good friends with their priest, Father Gayland Pool. Gayland invited me to work with the lectors at St. Luke's in the Meadow Episcopal Church. One Saturday afternoon I went with Joan and Joe to what we Baptists would call a cottage prayer meeting. Gayland baked the bread for the Eucharist. After he blessed it and broke it, the children served it. Then the cup was administered. This was one of the simplest but most meaningful services I have ever attended. Gayland helped me to understand that the problems in the Southern Baptist Convention were no different from those in the Episcopal church. He, Katie (his journalist wife), Joan, Joe, and a host of others were feeling the strain of being in one of the most reactionary Episcopal parishes in the country. Bishop Jack Iker refused to ordain women as priests or to allow them to have any significant role in the dioceses. He restricted Gayland in every way possible. Katie, with her journalistic skills and media connections, proved to be a constant irritation to the Bishop.

In October after Liz died in September, I attended a religious writers/speakers conference in Warm Beach, Washington. I received a grant to attend. I was not prepared to go anywhere, but God had more learning in store for me. Warm Beach is a beautiful place. In the woods overlooking Puget Sound, there is a small chapel where sunrise meditations are held. The setting alone was healing. On the last day of the conference, several of us had late flights from Seattle and decided to spend the day sightseeing together. One of the group members was an editor from Tyndale House

Publishers. Several weeks later I received a surprise gift from her, the book *Expect a Miracle*.[1] The premise of the book is that what happens to you is external. What you do with those events is internal. Every event can make you bitter or make you better. The choice is up to you. What a wonderful gift from someone whom I will never see again. That book and the thoughtfulness of the giver had a profound influence on my life. I continue to rely on those concepts and share them with others. I am convinced that God brings people into our lives when we most need them.

On another flight to Seattle to attend the national convention of the American Speech Language and Hearing association, I sat next to a gentleman on his way to Salt Lake City. As we talked, he assured me that I would see Liz again and that we would live together as a family. Of course, he was a member of the Church of Latter Day Saints. His concern and kindness were not just idle words. Several weeks later I received a package from him containing a warm note and a copy of *The Book of Mormon* . . . It made me uncomfortable to realize that I have never sent anyone other than family members a Bible. Step by agonizing step, I was learning to connect the vignettes in my life. The lessons kept coming from the most unexpected sources. Growth happens slowly and in unexpected ways. Perhaps that is by design so that we don't have a chance to erect our defenses.

I was dead. Just as dead as if I had been the one who died. I was desperate to do something, to accomplish something, to conquer something on my own to prove to myself that I was still alive. I was driving on empty and grasping for help. I expressed to my friend, Nancy Cash that I would like to learn to ballroom dance, not realizing the consequences of that casual remark. Nancy told her neighbor Ruth, an accomplished gold medal dancer. Ruth called me and offered to pick me up on her way to dance class. In a forceful but gentle way, she called my bluff. I went. I enrolled.

At the dance studio, the friendliest, most encouraging group of people greeted me. My first dance instructor was beautiful, willowy, charming, and far too patient and kind. She was the most

1. Galloway, *Expect a Miracle*.

graceful person on the dance floor I had ever seen. I was hooked. I worked hard to learn and to please her. I was a terrible student. I did not know that there was so much to learn, and I have less rhythm than a brick wall. That said, I was having fun and making wonderful new friends. I loved the waltz, did fairly well with swing, and adored the tango. I learned the rumba steps but not the body movement. I am far too inhibited to sway.

I attended the parties. Sometimes I would summon up the courage to ask Ruth to dance, but this was too painful for both of us. After about a year, I read about a dance camp and competition in Yarmoth, Massachusetts. I talked to Ruth. She would be visiting her family in New York City but would go for the weekend. This was my big challenge. I screwed up my courage and made reservations. I flew to Providence and took a bus to Yarmoth. I was truly on my own.

I enrolled in the classes and then entered the competition without knowing that I needed a partner. As I stood in the middle of that floor feeling like a bumpkin, the president of the local dance club came out to dance with me. She was delightful, and we did very well. It is still hard for me to believe that I actually did this. I think it was the most courageous act of my life. It was one of those defining moments. What did I have to lose?

Although no one would ever confuse me with a dancer, I was a pretty good sport. Women would ask me to dance, and a group of us became close friends. I rarely had to ask for a ride. We joined the amateur dance club, and we danced regularly at a couple of hotels. I was dancing several nights a week and taking swimming lessons. I was anxious about my ability, but I was having the time of my life. I was getting my life back.

What part was this playing in my spiritual development? What does dancing have to do with my discovering who God is? I was being brought back to life. I was discovering that I was still a capable person, and God was bringing wonderful people into my life. As my brother-in-law, Joe, would often say, "I was broadening my horizons." I desperately needed to know that I was still alive. I was trying something very different for me. Even though I was meeting with mediocre success on the dance floor, I was reentering life. It had very little to do with dance and everything to do with recapturing a zest for living. I could function as a single person, and it kept my mind occupied. The people I met were part of a new life. They didn't know Liz, and they had not known Liz and me as a couple. I had to do this on my own.

I met Arla Holroyd, a retired teacher from Rock Hill, South Carolina, at the amateur dance club. I am sure that it was Arla and her pastor at the French Protestant Huguenot Church, Phil Bryant, who recommended that the organ being given to Mt. Hermon RUME Church be given in honor of my service to the community. Bennett Bozart, a retired judge from New Jersey, developed the hobby of donating refurbished organs to churches that could not afford to buy one. He gave away more than 200. It was a marvelous dedication service. Phil said some glowing things about me. The Gospel Choir from the Medical University of South Carolina sang. The church was packed. It reminded me of a similar event many years earlier when the Jewish Community of Charleston recognized me for helping one of the Russian refugees they had brought to Charleston. The lessons just kept coming, or as Dr. Scott Walker would say, God keeps opening windows as to who he is.

9

Surrender

THROUGH HEROIC EFFORTS ON the part of many people, both local and across the country, the Speech and Hearing Center survived the ravages of Hurricane Hugo and its terrible aftermath late in September of 1989. Hugo probably taught us more about our dependence on one another than any other single event in my life. Although the center building received no damage, our clients were devastated. Even though we operated on a sliding fee scale, people who had been able to pay something before Hugo were now unable to do so. Donations came into our United Way from across the country, and the National Student Speech and Hearing Association adopted our center as its national project after I spoke at their meeting.

Hugo occurred on September 21, just after Liz died on September 4. One of our staff members confided to our bookkeeper, "We can't survive. Mitch is in no condition to lead us."

What happened was nothing short of a miracle. The center made a marvelous recovery, and the board and staff decided it was time to move to new and more spacious facilities.

After the center moved to our new building in 1991, the economy took a nosedive. The Charleston Naval Base was shut down after ninety-nine years of glorious service. Money at the center was in short supply and dwindling fast. I did everything I knew how to do, but finally I realized that I had exhausted my bag of tricks. The board of directors and staff turned over every stone

Surrender

they could find. There was only one avenue left to me, and that was the hardest. I knew that I had to surrender everything to God.

I prayed over and over again, "God, you know that the hardest thing for me to do is to let go. You know that I am a control freak. Please help me let go. This is a wonderful program, but if you want it saved, you will have to save it. I've done everything I know to do. It's up to you."

It wasn't an easy prayer, but gradually the load lifted. I felt more and more able to cope. Board members and staff members were as supportive as they could be. Instead of assigning blame, they sought ways to help and support me. Over and over they asked, "What can we do to help you?" It is impossible to adequately relate the position of this agency in the community. They are such a part of each other. Later in the year, because of changes in government regulations, the Trident United Way decided to end our long-standing retirement program for which it was the administrator and to distribute the funds as prescribed in the agreement. After all the individuals were paid their shares, the Speech and Hearing Center was left with thousands of dollars that we didn't know we had. The money was there all along. Coincidence—maybe, but you'll never convince me that it wasn't the answer to prayer. That's what a father does. He looks after his children. It had to be a miracle because there was nothing more I could do without divine intervention. The board of directors and the staff worked hard and pulled together. There was no blame game—no finger pointing. The miracles kept coming. I knew without a doubt that I was in the right place and that I was doing what God wanted me to do. To work harmoniously with a changing board of directors for thirty-five years is a miracle in itself, but to have their support through such a crisis is amazing. I will never cease to be grateful for the opportunity I had to serve this agency and this community for so long. If it is possible to have a thirty-five year honeymoon with an organization and with a city, then I had one.

Without my knowledge, a big celebration had been planned for my twenty-fifth anniversary at the center. Unfortunately, the date fell during the time Liz was in the hospital. The surprise party

Our Father

was held in the waiting room of St. Francis Hospital. When I said that I was going to show the plaque to Liz in intensive care, they said, "She has already seen it. She knows all about it." These were wonderful people who truly cared about us. Love like that doesn't just happen. I was more convinced than ever that God had brought us to Charleston. I am grateful to him for these people every day of my life. They demonstrated to my family what "Our Father" really means during our hours of greatest need.

10

New Beginnings

I WAS SINGLE AGAIN for nine years before Carol and I were married at First Baptist Church in Charleston. Not by any stretch of the imagination did I ever think that I would marry again. I was so devastated by the loss of Liz. Our good Catholic friends, Germaine and John Carney, brought Carol and me together. Germaine knew that we were both Baptists and assumed that all Baptists were the same. I had lectured at the University of South Carolina, and the Carneys invited me to have dinner with them. On the way to their home, Germaine said casually, "Oh, by the way, I have also invited one of my fellow teachers to eat with us." Germaine had asked Carol to bring one of her famous almond pound cakes for dessert. During dessert she wrote on a napkin and handed it to Carol. "Give Mitch some pound cake to take home with him." Naturally I had to call and thank her. She rode with the Carneys when they drove me back to the bus station for my trip home. She knew from the beginning that I did not drive because of my poor vision. Germaine had already filled her in on most of the details of my life. Germaine was convinced that we belonged together.

Carol and a group of her friends planned a weekend in Charleston. Carol came ahead of the group on a Friday night so that we could meet for dinner. The friends then decided to bow out of the weekend. Unfortunately, I already had plans for Saturday night; therefore, I invited her to have breakfast at the St. John's Island Café on Saturday morning. During that breakfast, I realized that I was relaxed, comfortable, and talking easily with this stranger. When I glanced at my watch, I could hardly believe how long we had been there. At that moment I knew that perhaps life wasn't over. Leaving her alone to fend for herself on Saturday night was awkward, but I assured myself that her friends were to blame. I think they set me up.

Sunday afternoon we walked on Folly Beach and talked and talked. She was still suffering from a terrible divorce after twenty years of marriage, and I was still in mourning. This was a new beginning, and we both sensed it. Our relationship developed slowly. I continued to go out with other women, but now they were all compared to Carol. I made more and more trips to Columbia, and she made more and more trips to Charleston. Our telephone bills skyrocketed.

Joyce and Bennett Murray are close friends. After Liz died, they continued to invite me to go out to eat with them. I rode with Bennett every Tuesday to Optimist Club meetings and many other functions. On Sunday mornings, he and I sat together in church. Joyce sings in the choir. I thought it was a little strange when Bennett called one day to make an appointment to go out to eat. I was totally unprepared for what lay ahead. After a little of our good-natured foolishness, things became very quiet. Bennett took me into his confidence, telling me that he was dying of cancer. He also exacted my promise not to tell anyone, as he didn't want to elicit any sympathy. As the months wore on and his health declined, this promise became harder and harder to keep. He tried to keep up appearances, but it became more and more difficult. Mutual friends knew that I knew the real story, but somehow I managed to keep my promise.

At the 1993 Christmas Eve service at First Baptist, Bennett requested an opportunity to speak to the congregation. To say that his testimony was traumatic would be a gross understatement. There was absolute silence. Bennett was the most popular member of the congregation. After that night he was in and out of the hospital for chemotherapy treatments and blood transfusions. We talked often and candidly about what lay ahead. He was not concerned for

New Beginnings

himself, only for Joyce and their two children, Michael and Michelle. His great, unorthodox sense of humor never wavered.

When I went to the hospital late one afternoon, I had no way of knowing that it was the last time I would see him. Before I left, the family had gathered, but I did not sense that this was the end. I went with the family to make arrangements for his funeral, and I was honored when they asked me to read the "Optimist Creed" at his graveside.[1]

Bennett and I were closer than close. He had a wonderful sense of humor that knew no bounds. He often asked to introduce me when I was to make a speech. I never would agree because I was not sure that I would be able to recover enough to go on with my talk. He could brighten the dullest meeting and often did. Once again there was an empty seat beside me in church on Sunday mornings, but it does not compare with the empty spot he left in my heart. I miss his friendship, his laughter, his zany telephone calls, his sound reasoning in church meetings, his boundless faith, and his encouragement.

I received a birthday card that year with a return address of Bennett Murray, "Heaven." Joyce found the card in Bennett's things and knew that he had intended it for me. Like Bennett, Joyce has a terrific sense of humor.

In a few short years, death had claimed my father, mother, wife, and best friend, and yet I was still here. The only reasonable conclusion I could come to was that God must have something left for me to do or learn, or why else would I still be here? No other explanation made any sense. I prayed earnestly that I would discover his purpose for my remaining years. I discovered a wonderful article in *Leadership Magazine* by Gordon MacDonald that provided much needed guidance. In "What I Want to Be When I Grow Up," he urged that each of us develop a mission statement for our remaining years and provided forceful arguments for doing so.[2] It is not an easy process to go through but more than worth

---

1. "The Optimist Creed," *Optimist International*, www.optimist.org/creed.cfm, (8 March, 2015).

2. MacDonald, "What I Want To Be When I Grow Up," 68.

the effort. I worked on mine for months. I recommend the exercise to anyone. MacDonald cautioned that without a plan, many older people become very poor company for themselves and others.

I would like to share my personal Mission Statement:

> To continue to develop intellectually, spiritually, emotionally, physically, and financially in order to function as an enthusiastic, positive, cheerful, healthy, productive, and resourceful member of my family, church, profession, and community.

11

Playing God and Failing Miserably

DURING THIS TIME I experienced another spiritual, emotional, near-death experience that was almost as painful as the loss of Liz and Bennett. My beloved First Baptist Church turned on itself and fractured in all directions. A large group eventually formed a new church, Providence Baptist Church. Other members became Presbyterian and Episcopalian. A few simply stopped attending church anywhere and became very bitter.

As a congregation, we never dealt with our pain over the tragedy of Henry Finch. We united briefly to repair the tremendous damages caused by Hurricane Hugo in 1989. We struggled to keep the controversy in the Southern Baptist Convention from invading the church. I was a member of a study group designated to sift through the issues dividing the convention, and the group did its work diligently. However, in the end, the deacons voted that our report should not be presented to the congregation. In my opinion, that was a terrible mistake. Our pastor, Scott Walker, left to become pastor of the First Baptist Church in Waco, Texas. Many people resented his connections to the Cooperative Baptist Fellowship, a moderate group, and accused him of wanting to take First Baptist Church out of the Southern Baptist Convention. Some even absurdly accused him of not believing the Bible.

Many people on both sides of the issues worked tirelessly to keep the church together. We were no match for those who were trying to force the dissenters out or for those who wanted to form their own church. The newly formed Cooperative Baptist Fellowship became the scapegoat for the controversy, but, in reality, it was nothing more than an old-fashioned power struggle—a family fight. I thought that I was being a part of the solution, but I ended up being a part of the problem. I thought wrongly that God was relying on me to help save his church. What arrogance! I thought that God needed me when the real problem was that I needed God. I have sought forgiveness from people that I disappointed and wounded and most of all from God. Mervyn Gibson probably said it better than anyone. "During the ministry of Dr. Scott Walker, our church was probably as near an ideal as a church can get. The devil just couldn't stand it any longer and tore it apart."

A long-time friend, but on the other side of the struggle from me, said, "Mitch, all of the supposed troublemakers have gone, but things are no better. Some people just like to fight."

When a search committee was elected by the congregation to find a new pastor, the committee was evenly divided. We were so polarized that we were unable to elect a chairperson. We elected a secretary. One member was so hostile that he refused to sit in a circle with the rest of us. He sat at a desk and faced sideways during the first couple of meetings. In order to begin the process, someone suggested that the committee members must resolve some of their own issues before we could adequately represent the church. Cindy Keys suggested that we each give our own testimony of our journey of faith and that we pray for each other by name daily. This took several weeks but was a wonderful experience as we learned of each other's struggles.

I can't speak for anyone except myself, but I could not stay angry with a person and pray for him or her at the same time. This was an eye-opening, soul-stretching, and faith-building experience. The committee gradually came together and worked harmoniously. The bitterness that had been so pervasive melted away. We presented a unanimous recommendation to the congregation. Dr. Lamar King was called to be our pastor with less than a half dozen negative votes from the entire congregation. It was a triumph of prayer. Perhaps we use the term "miracle" too freely, but in my mind this was a miracle. People who did not want to be in the same room with one another when we started came together as a result of prayer. It was thrilling!

Unfortunately we stopped praying and working too soon. Most of us thought that we had done our job and done it well, but less than a year later, Dr. King was sacrificed on the same old altar of control. It is impossible to describe the agony of this experience. It was evident to all concerned that lots of work remained to be done, but there was also no mistaking the fact that the most conservative group in the congregation was now in control. Raymond Langlois, an experienced and respected conservative minister from Tennessee was called as interim pastor. It was during his tenure that I experienced my darkest moment in the struggle. My former professor and friend, Jack Porter, was traveling with two young missionaries trained at the Baptist Seminary in Ruschikon, Switzerland, and now relocated to Prague. He wanted to arrange a speaking opportunity for them in Charleston. When I approached Raymond about this, he readily agreed. I reminded him that the Southern Baptists Convention had withdrawn its financial support from the seminary. He said, "Missionaries are missionaries." I was uneasy about his quick response and waited two or three weeks to invite the group. My misgivings served me well. Raymond sent me a letter withdrawing his invitation. He could have told me in person on Sunday morning or telephoned me, but he chose to write a letter. This action told me all I needed to know. Providence Baptist Church readily agreed to invite the young couple to speak, and they did a marvelous job. I did not challenge Raymond's actions because the church had experienced more than our share of problems. Later in private conversations, he told me that he had been told by the leadership that all those who thought the way I do had left the church. I said, "Raymond, all we wanted was for you to throw us a bone." He answered, "Mitch, I didn't have a bone to throw to you. My mission was to save this church."

His agony was apparent, for he and I had truly enjoyed a good relationship. I knew that he loved First Baptist Church and was struggling to hold it together. He has returned to visit several times and is always warmly received. After being at the church for only a few weeks, he preached a sermon in which he stated that his observation was that we were predominantly a conservative congregation. I had been a member for over thirty years at that time, and I would not have ventured such an evaluation. More people left. I could not bring myself to leave a fellowship that had been so caring for my children and me during our time of suffering. My love for the church is too deep. My roots are too entwined. Even with all the struggles we have gone through, this is still the warmest, friendliest fellowship I have ever experienced. I know that if I had a great personal need, I could go to the member of the congregation with whom I have disagreed the most, and that need would be met if it were within his or her power to do so. The fellowship is unbelievable. I can't explain it other than to say that this is a congregation that loves each other, and that love takes precedence over every other issue.

I believe that you cannot influence an organization or a denomination from the outside. You must be a team player. I have seen this played out in the public school system in my beloved Charleston, where the wealthier and more influential members of the community have deserted the public schools, thus ensuring the failure of those schools. The affluent then cite those failures as their reason for leaving, but they surrendered their ability to change them. This principle of withdrawal works the same way with any organization.

Carol and I were married at First Baptist on July 25, 1998. Our wedding served as a reunion. Many of those who had left the church came back for the first time. Two of them took an active role. Dr. Tom Guerry was one of our ministers, and Dianna McBroom sang "The Lord's Prayer." Everyone was having a great time and once again enjoying fellowship with one another. The reception in the fellowship hall was bursting with laughter and good cheer. Guests lingered for a long time. Not only were Carol and I joined in matrimony, but also many old friendships began the healing process. Truly the hymn is correct, "Surely the Lord is in This Place."

Playing God and Failing Miserably

Both congregations are now flourishing and doing great works. Both bare the scars that only a family conflict can inflict, when neither is yet able to deal with the collective pain nor move toward reconciliation as institutions, but many individuals have renewed their friendships. Some former choir members have returned to sing on special occasions. The process has been extremely painful, but through it I have learned once again that God can use our horrible man-made messes for his purposes. Good can come from evil, but it doesn't just happen. It requires work, prayer, and divine intervention. I am not trying to minimize the consequences of this conflict or gloss over the horrendous pain that it caused. The pain was not only ours at First Baptist, but it was also played out in church after church across the country. The Southern Baptists Convention that I had known from childhood was destroyed, and a new structure arose with the same name but bearing no resemblance to the one I had known. The convention that had nourished me in so many ways was gone and now vilified many of the saints that I revered.

During all of this time, one factor at First Baptist remained constant and reassuring—the music. David Redd, minister of music and worship, was not only one of the most outstanding church organists to be found; he was also a gentleman and an artistic genius. The music is best described as classical. "I have an agreement with Willie Nelson. If he won't play my organ, I won't play his guitar."

There is no way to overstate David's influence or the importance of the music program. It is the tie that binds our hearts. David died unexpectedly in February 2001. No congregation ever experienced a greater loss. No matter what the controversies were, the beauty of the sanctuary, the sounds of the magnificent organ, a talented choir, and the formal service made worship paramount. For at least a little while, you knew why you were in church. You were there to worship. A memorial service for David brought back musicians who had worked with him and had scattered to many congregations. It was truly a celebration of his life. The church was packed. As I have struggled to sort through all of this, I have come to realize that through First Baptist, with the influence of David Redd and Dr. John Hamrick, I have learned how to worship. I came knowing how to thank God, how to praise God, and how to pray, but what I have learned is how to worship God. Evangelism is important and emphasized, but worship is central to mature one's faith. David kept the focus on worship. From the first day that Liz and I walked into that sanctuary, we knew we were at home. I still feel that way, and so does Carol.

From this struggle I have slowly come to the conviction that whether we are fundamentalists, conservatives, moderates, or liberals, we are still God's children. It's a part of our childish nature to fight with one another, but that is not the way mature Christians should conduct themselves. If I claim the doctrine of the priesthood of the individual believer or soul competency for myself, I must be willing to grant it to others. This is easy to say but hard to live. Because I do not see the burning bush, that doesn't mean that you don't see it or experience it. Sometimes growth is extremely painful.

12

Grace upon Grace

I DON'T KNOW WHEN I first heard of the Chautauqua Institution in western New York State. Perhaps it was at Mars Hill College, but I nourished a passion to go there. My friend, Joan Solomon, from my Furman days suggested that I submit a proposal to teach a course in its special studies program. Joan now lives in Rochester, New York, and spends the entire summer at Chautauqua working on the daily newspaper staff. I followed her suggestion, and when my proposal to teach a workshop on personal development was accepted, I was overjoyed.

My journey of faith has quickened by the outstanding speakers I hear at Chautauqua and the many conversations with new friends. On my first visit, I stayed at the denominational house operated by the United Church of Christ and was invited by its chaplain, Don Skinner, to participate in administering communion with a member of that faith and my Catholic friend, Joan Solomon. What a moving experience. It was another step on my journey. Joan introduced me to a tremendous number of her friends and institute staff members on that first visit.

Dr. Linda Bridges, a theology professor now at Wake Forest University, was the chaplain of the week. What a profound story she had to tell. She lost her job at Southern Baptist Theological Seminary in Louisville because "women should not teach men theology." What a terrible perversion of the Scriptures. Linda grew up around Greer, South Carolina, the daughter of a mountain preacher. One of her messages that week that has stuck with me dealt with how we are the recipients of grace upon grace. I think of her explanation often because the reception of grace upon grace describes my life more fully than any other way I can express. Linda was well received by all who attended. Joan and I met her for lunch one day to explore our South Carolina roots. We had a great time swapping stories and getting to know each other's spiritual journey more fully.

The religion speaker for the week in the Hall of Philosophy was Dr. Loren Mead, director of the Alban Institute, a group that works with troubled churches. He is also a South Carolinian. He offered sound guidance on trying to understand and deal with the radical turn of events in the Southern Baptist Convention and in my own congregation. "Stay as long as it nourishes you," he counseled. He also emphasized that the struggles we were having are not unique to Southern Baptists, but are taking place throughout all religious groups. He echoed the same thoughts as Gayland Pool, the Episcopal priest in Texas.

This first visit to Chautauqua was more than I could ever have expected. I felt so at home. I felt somehow as if I had been preparing for this adventure my entire life. I could hardly wait to return. In fact, I seriously considered applying for a staff position.

Carol was with me on my second visit. My misgivings about whether or not she would share my enthusiasm for Chautauqua proved to be totally unfounded. She loved the experience as much as I do. We heard wonderful messages from Dr. John Claypool, a former Southern Baptist turned Episcopalian, Dr. Renita J. Weems, a black female Hebrew scholar from the Divinity School at Vanderbilt University, and Dr. Martin Marty. Claypool gave a series of messages on the lives of seven disciples. They were based on something his grandfather taught him. "Anyone can learn from his/her own experience, but a wise person learns from the experiences of others." Each message took me further than I have ever been with new insights into what it means to be Christian. Especially meaningful is his paraphrased quote from St. Augustine that, "God loves all of us as he loves each of us, and he loves each of us as he loves all of us."[1] Carol and I were early for every lecture—a minor miracle.

Martin Marty shared a broad and rich tapestry of religious history, making sense out of events that had never made sense before. His theme stressed that if religion has the power to kill, it also has the power to heal. He was very gracious, especially when I was trying to persuade him to be a speaker for the Hamrick Lectureship held in Charleston. Carol had one of his books in her hand. He noticed it and offered to autograph it and inscribed it to both of us. Here was someone who is in demand everywhere but takes the time to be gracious to strangers. We were struck with the fact that this world-renowned scholar is still a parish priest at heart.

Dr. Weems forced us to look at our concepts about women in general and black women in particular. She used the overwhelmingly white demographics of the Chautauqua Institution attendees to make her point.

Joan Solomon writes a column for the *Chautauqua Daily*, recounting the sermon of the previous day. Sometimes she also interviews the speaker. She has such a tremendous ability to capture the essence of the message and to focus attention on the really important points. Her writings contribute to the total experience. I am always eager to read what she has written about the sermon. I have urged her to collect all of her columns into a book. She truly has a gift for capturing the message.

One of our recent visits was no less meaningful. Dr. Cynthia Campbell, president of McCormick Theological Seminary in Chicago, challenged our traditional thinking. She delivered the most moving and insightful sermon on the crucifixion I have ever heard. She also echoed the thoughts of my childhood pastor, Preacher Gowan, by stating, "There is no question that you can ask that God hasn't already thought about. There is no thought or topic that can threaten God. There is no place you can go where God is not already there."

---

1. "Saint Augustine Quotes," *Brainy Quotes*, http://www.brainyquote.com/quotes/authors/s/saint_augustine.html, (12 March 2015).

Our Father

We had a great time renewing our friendship with Dr. Molly Marshall, who is a professor of Spiritual Formations at Central Baptist Theological Seminary in Kansas, where she now serves as president. She pushed us hard when she discussed the presence and workings of the Holy Spirit during an evening service at the Baptist House. Dr. Marshall spoke at the Hamrick Lectureship and left a lasting impression. Our current pastor continues to quote her. We met Dr. Alton M. Motter, a 94-year-old Lutheran minister who has been a tireless worker on behalf of ecumenicalism and was in attendance at Vatican Two. What an inspiration!

Chautauqua symbolizes for me my growing realization of what "Our Father" really means. The program challenges me to think, to meditate, to explore, and to move beyond my spiritual safety zone. Because there are so many others there who are wrestling with many of the same issues and who are willing to share their experiences, the learning comes quicker, but no less painfully. You can just be walking along the path after a lecture or drinking coffee at the Presbyterian House and strike up a conversation with a total stranger and gain a totally new insight. When I was an undergraduate at Mars Hill College, classmates would speak of their experience at Ridgecrest Baptist Assembly as a mountain top experience. Chautauqua is my mountain top experience. I can hardly wait to go back. Insights come from unexpected sources. In a discussion during a writing seminar, I was lamenting the battles we Southern Baptists have when a member of another denomination spoke up. "I admire you Baptists," she said. "At least you care. In my denomination, no one seems to care about anything." I had not thought about it in those terms. Her observation does put another face on the denominational aspect of faith.

During a memoir writing workshop taught by Marion Roach Smith, she asked me, "Mitch, how do you talk to God?" I answered, "I talk to God just as I am talking to you." Her reply, "Then write that. Let us feel it." In fact, I talk to God hundreds of times a day about everything and anything that crosses my path.

I know that Chautauqua is so meaningful for me because of all the other experiences I have had. The grounding I received at Northside Baptist Church, the influence of Christian teachers, the years of teaching Sunday school, and the many pastors I have heard prepared the way. I also know that I must be open to new insights and different points of view. The inspiration and insights I gain there enrich my life and deepen my spiritual journey.

13

Friends and Mentors

I TAUGHT AN ADULT Sunday school class at First Baptist Church for more than twenty-five years. It was really a discussion class. I presented a short introduction, speaking for perhaps ten or fifteen minutes, and then opened the floor for discussion. What marvelous discussions they were! The class members became a family. Members were free to explore any area and any thoughts without fear. For most of us, it was a unique experience. I know that I gained more than any other member of the class. I began each year with the premise that if you are coming here for answers, there are none. Our goal is to end each year with a better set of questions than those with which we started. It usually worked out that way, and the struggle was more than worth the effort.

Perhaps the most unusual experience we had was to have a series of dialogues with a group of secular humanists. We met in different homes over a period of months. No one changed his or her position, but we all gained new insights. The encounters challenged us who are Christians to wrestle with our own beliefs and to talk about them in clear, understandable terms. It was surprising to find some areas of agreement and heart warming to build bridges where none had been before.

A Reformed rabbi visiting in Charleston from New York, whom I invited to speak to the class after reading about him in the newspaper, taught the most memorable Sunday school lesson. "If you are serious about following the teachings of Jesus Christ," he said, "you had better learn something about Jewish history. You will be the most persecuted group on earth because Jesus was a radical, and his teachings are radical."

When Liz's parents were in town, they attended Sunday school with me. The members loved them, especially her farther, Dr. Frei. He entered into the discussions and shared his vast experience, but he did not always say what one expected. He had a world view with a historical perspective that undergirded his faith. His sense of humor was contagious, and he was an incurable punster. Discussions of the morning's lesson continued at home and often into the evening. He loved the formality of the worship service at First Baptist Church because this was not his experience with other Baptists he had known and with whom he had worked. He was one of the founders of the language school for missionaries in the Philippines. At first the Southern Baptists did not want to cooperate because the Roman Catholics were involved, but when the other groups did not knuckle under to their threat to withdraw, the Baptists joined and cooperated. Mrs. Frei was much more reserved and much more conservative in her beliefs. She sometimes was uncomfortable in the discussions and would often challenge her husband's liberalism. Our class did not conform to her ideas about who Baptists were. On the other hand, he was at home and enjoyed the give and take. He respected the ideas of each class member and in turn enjoyed their appreciation of his experience. He knew how to gently challenge.

One day I asked him to explain the concept of predestination to me. "Mitch," he said, "Predestination should only be discussed by theologians and rarely by them because the theology is so misunderstood and, thus, controversial." He was a remarkable man who had witnessed all the horrors that men can inflict on one another during the Japanese occupation of the Philippines, and, through it all, could still demonstrate a faith that was contagious.

I have the rare privilege of meeting for lunch once each month with wonderful friends, Dr. Tom Guerry, professor of religion at Charleston Southern University; Dr. Monty Knight, pastor of the First Christian Church, Disciples of Christ, and formerly the director of the Summerville, South Carolina, Mental Health Clinic; and Dr. Scott McBroom, an ordained Baptist minister, who is also a mental health counselor. From time to time, we invite a guest to share our discussions. We began these when Lamar King was pastor of First Baptist in order to introduce him to the community. We enjoyed them so much that we continued even after Lamar left. We explore every angle of our Christian experiences, our philosophies, our frustrations, our disappointments, our attitudes, and our assumptions. All of us have been deeply wounded by the fundamentalist take-over of the Southern Baptist Convention. No question or comment is off limits or free from in-depth scrutiny. I am the layperson in the group, which gives me the opportunity to ask the questions that are troubling me. I am not always prepared for, or comfortable with, the answers I get, but the discussions fill such a deep need for me. I often wonder why there aren't more groups like this in which you can risk sharing your deepest thoughts without fear of being put down, ridiculed, or consigned to hell. Our discussions are often interrupted by someone seated at a nearby table who overhears a part of the conversation and comes over to ask a question or challenge a remark. One of the waitresses sometimes pulls up a chair to listen after the lunch rush dies down.

These discussions have led to our attending the Lenten Lecture Series at Mepkin Abbey for the past several years. Here renowned Biblical scholars continue to push my understanding of what it means to be a member of the family of God. Abbott Francis Kline, a world-renowned organist, has been a very gracious host and has attended the Hamrick Lectureship at First Baptist. Years earlier Rev. Paul Pridgen Jr. and the former Abbott started a Baptist/Catholic dialogue. To some degree, we are keeping it going. Besides being a place for intellectual and spiritual growth, Mepkin Abbey also occupies one of the most beautiful sites in the world on the banks of the Cooper River.

For several summers, I taught a special graduate course dealing with the not-for-profit sector and its importance to our daily lives. As a part of this, I take the students to Congregation Beth Elohim, the birthplace of Reformed Judaism in America. Through this I have gained so many understandings from Rabbi Anthony Holz. I owe a great debt to him and to Stuart Cohen and Skippy Weil. When my Optimist Club sold Christmas trees as a fundraiser, Skippy worked right along with the rest of us. Recently Skippy asked me, "Mitch, do Christians still believe that we (Jews) killed Jesus?" We have a lot of work to do.

Stuart and I worked together at the Speech and Hearing Center for twenty-two years. We had hundreds of religious discussions during those years. I also attended a Seder (Jewish Passover meal) and Stuart's son's bar mitzvah. These experiences helped further my understanding of the Jewish roots of Christianity, and they make reading the Scriptures an even richer experience.

Rabbi Holz was unbelievably gracious one morning when a graduate student asked, "Are you telling us that Jews do not believe in Jesus?" He displayed the same marvelous tact when asked by a student about the struggles then taking place at First Baptist. "It's just their turn in the barrel," he said. "Let me tell you about some of our struggles."

Over the past several years, I have reveled in a growing friendship with Dr. John A. Hamrick, pastor of First Baptist Church for twenty-nine years and the founding president of the Baptist College of Charleston, now Charleston Southern. His breadth of understanding, his acceptance of other points of view, and his intense love of and dedication to God are inspiring. "If God tells you to do something, he will find a way for you to do it. Nothing is impossible with God."

It was his admonition that, "If we Baptists knew our history, we would never have let what happened to the Southern Baptist Convention happen," that inspired me to promote and chair the annual John A. Hamrick Lectureship in Baptist History. It is really church history, but former state senator Charles Gibson taught me years earlier that politics is the science of the possible.

The lectureship has brought outstanding church history scholars to its platform. Each has caused me to think and study more, but perhaps none more than Dr. Molly Marshall, who focused on spiritual formations. She drew on the experiences of other religious groups, especially the monastic societies. She is another female theologian who felt the wrath of the new leadership in the Southern Baptist Convention. She became an instant favorite at First Baptist. The congregation fell in love with her.

When Liz and I joined First Baptist Church in 1964, Dr. Hamrick said to Liz, "I am going to ask you this only once because it is my responsibility to ask you. Do you have any interest in becoming a Southern Baptist?"

"No," she said, "I don't."

"Welcome to the church," he said. "The only thing you can't do is to vote to give it to the Presbyterians."

With those words, he earned my gratitude and respect. I knew we were in the right place. Liz felt to change denominations would be a repudiation of the work of her parents. Dr. John, as we affectionately called Dr. Hamrick, understood that and never raised the question again. She was a member of the church in every sense of the word. Her name even appeared on the membership rolls for possible election as a deacon. No one remembered or cared that she was still a Presbyterian, at least officially. Her Presbyterian heritage would shine through bright and clear when I fretted about some missed opportunity. "Don't worry, honey," she would say. "If it is to be, it will be."

Another of Dr. John's great contributions came about during the annual religious emphasis weeks, when some renowned minister would conduct a series of meetings. One of the most popular features of these was a noon luncheon for local business people, which included a kosher table. This gesture of friendship was extremely well received and remembered by the business community to this day. It is no wonder that the Jewish community was very supportive of his efforts to found the Baptist College of Charleston. "We are not Christians, but we want to live in a community with Christian principles."

Many years later I asked him, "Dr. John, when you stand in the First Baptist pulpit to preach, does it make you nervous to think about all of the renowned preachers who have preached here?"

"Mitch, it did at first," he said, "but, then I realized that I didn't have to please Richard Furman. I only have to please God."

Dr. John and I have discussed so many things. Each time we converse, I come away with a richer understanding and renewed determination to go further. He never tires of answering my questions or explaining some theological concept to me. His faith and his broad acceptance of those who differ with him are truly encouraging.

Each summer for several years, I asked him to speak to the graduate class I teach at Webster University that deals with the "not-for-profit" sector because religious institutions play such a large part. His lecture on the founding of the Baptist College of Charleston is truly amazing and inspiring. It is really the story of miracles on top of miracles. After his lecture in the summer of 1997, as we were driving to lunch at the Harbor Club, he launched into a different lecture. He told me how God had given him two wonderful wives and that God's plan was not for man to live alone. He talked about his late wife, Margaret, and then sang the praises of his current wife, Jane, "She is my Marilyn Monroe." He didn't stop there. He told me what an attractive, charming woman Carol is. When I got home I telephoned Jane and asked her why she had turned Dr. John loose on me.

"I didn't do it," she protested. "That was his idea."

Of course, Carol and I were thrilled to have him take a major role in our wedding ceremony. What could be more fitting?

During the years of the Clinton administration, I became more and more concerned about the attacks on the president personally and on Hillary and even on Chelsea by the religious right. In the aftermath of the Lewinski affair, I was horrified by the wrath heaped upon him and the lack of forgiveness by fundamentalist Christians. They seemed to have either forgotten or totally corrupted the teachings of Scripture, especially those of Jesus concerning forgiveness. They seemed to revel in the president's wrongdoing.

The president said that he had asked God for forgiveness, and he asked the people for forgiveness. Where was the spirit of love? I received scandalous e-mails concerning the president from those who professed to be Christian. When I reminded them about not spreading gossip, they sent even more. It seems to me that we are Christian because we have been forgiven. "For in the same way you judge others, you will be judged, and with the measure you use, it will be measured to you" (Matt. 7:2 NIV).

At any rate, the scandal and the extreme reactions to it caused me to look again at some of those great flawed heroes in the Bible and how God used them to spread his truth and demonstrate his great love for us. Look at Moses, David, and Paul. I am not equating Bill Clinton with those Bible heroes, but if God can use their lives for good, why should we doubt that he would forgive and use the former president?

I use a lot of case studies in my graduate classes, and I always ask the students, "Why is this particular case in the textbook?" David is a great case study in The Book, but one can ask the same question. Why is this case here? David did not fall into sin. He wasn't lured into sin. No, David joyfully leaped into sin and reveled in it. But God did not wash his hands of David. He rescued him, and the Scriptures tell us that David was a man after God's own heart. Had all of these pious voices forgotten the story of David? Just because we are not powerful or famous does not make our sins any less grievous to him. However, God does not wash his hands of us when we sin.

It seemed to me that the religious right used its considerable media connections and its collective shrill voice to rejoice in evildoing. There was no restraint. There was no understanding of the stewardship of Christian communication, a concept beautifully outlined by Dr. Quentin J. Schultze in his outstanding book, *Communicating for Life*. Jerry Falwell and Pat Robertson repeated and compounded their mistakes of uncontrolled verbal venom during the Clinton era after the tragedy of September 11. Dr. Schultze's book is the best I have ever read on responsible Christian communication.

My grandchildren, Christina and Colin, took part in the Christmas pageant at the Unitarian Church in Charleston. Christina joined the other angels, a most appropriate place for her.

Four-year-old Colin wanted to be a dog at the manger and was permitted to do so. He made a wonderful dog in his costume, complete with ears and a tail. I was impressed that not only did the Unitarians have a Christmas play, but that they allowed my grandson to be a dog. This is the kind of religious freedom that was such a part of my background as a Baptist. Of course, Jesus had a dog. I was thrilled to be there. I came home and wrote a story for Colin about the dog at the manger.

Dr. Thomas McKibbens, senior minister at Newton Center First Baptist Church in Newton, Massachusetts, was the lecturer for the Hamrick Lectureship in 2001. His message, "The Theology of Friendship," seemed to capture everything I had been thinking. He traced how friendships, in spite of differences, influenced the entire history of Baptists in America until this very day. He related how contributions from northern churches saved the struggling Southern Baptist Seminary after the Civil War. Their generosity was inspired by friendships. Friendship is more powerful than theology and even endured and survived the horrors of the Civil War.

Shells from Union forces destroyed the First Baptist Church pulpit designed by Robert Mills. Tom McKibbens is a descendant of Basal Manly, one of the early ministers of the church who preached from that pulpit. When Marshall Blalock, current pastor, gave McKibbens a piece of the wood salvaged from that pulpit, I realized that this was a gesture that said far more than words alone. McKibbens was taking this back to Boston, where it would be on display. Friendship is indeed stronger than hostility. McKibbens's lectures and attitude kindled an active desire with many of those present to try to establish relationships between our respective congregations and perhaps First Baptist Church in Boston, with whom we share such a great history. We are truly one people. McKibbens made our connections real. In addition to the lectures, he delivered the sermon on Sunday morning, and it was obvious to everyone present that he was at home in that pulpit.

Carol and I made a trip back to Huntington, West Virginia, in April 2001. We visited with her Uncle Raymond, her dad's brother. The third brother was a wild, unlettered holiness preacher who started a mission on Eighth Avenue. If I had met Leonard Spurlock during his lifetime, I would have judged him crazy or, at best, a fanatic several bricks shy of a load. I would not have gone within a mile of his mission, but as I read his self-published monograph, I became convinced of his absolute trust in God. As weird as he seemed to be, he had something. He believed with an unshakable fervor that God would supply all of his needs and the needs of all believers. I was reminded of the scene in the movie, "The Apostle," where Robert Duval is watching the Catholic priest baptize a parishioner and says, "You do it your way, and I do it mine, but we get the job done."[1] This unlettered man certainly knew the meaning of "Our Father."

Dr. Timothy Johnson, a Catholic theologian teaching at Emory University, said at one of the Lenten Lectures at Mepkin Abbey that we learn our theology in community. My experience would echo his remarks. A group of us have been having dinner together on Wednesday nights for twenty years. The group shrinks and expands, but three of us have been there for the entire time. Currently there are three Catholics, two Presbyterians, one Episcopalian, one Disciples of Christ, and two Baptists. We run the political gauntlet from right-wing Republican to liberal Democrat. We also are diverse geographically—two Yankees, five mid-westerners, and two southerners, but the fellowship is extraordinary. We celebrate birthdays and major holidays together. We try to arrange our schedules so as not to miss the Wednesday night gatherings. We include family members or guests when they are in town. Naturally we discuss everything. We have gained such an understanding of each other's beliefs by sharing in the high points and low ones in each other's lives. They were a rock of support when Liz died, and they continued to include me. They embraced Carol with open arms after we were married. Two of our members have since faced life threatening illnesses. These wonderful people are more than friends; they are family. Although from different backgrounds, all are believers, active in their various congregations,

1. *The Apostle,* directed by Robert Duvall (1998; USA: Universal Studios, 1998).

and all are respected and respectful of each other. The group is a small snapshot of what the Christian family could be. We have learned so much about each other's faith and have come to realize that we are all more alike than different and that the differences don't really matter.

Carol and I had a wonderful vacation to France in the summer of 2002. All that we saw entranced us like millions of other tourists. Even being pick-pocketed didn't spoil the magic. Neither of us will ever get over walking among the thousands of white crosses in the American Cemetery or walking over the battlegrounds at Normandy. Jane Hamrick told us of a "must visit" destination on our trip, and we followed her advice. When Carol and I stepped inside the Basilica Sacre Coeur in Paris, neither of us was prepared for the sensation of worship that flooded over us. The huge mosaic depicting Christ with outstretched arms is so real, so compelling, that you want to fall to your knees. Carol and I stood in awed silence, and then we sat for a long time without a word. When she did speak, Carol captured the essence of our experience. "Now that is the universal language! Everyone can understand that. All you want to do is worship."

In January 2008 Carol and I along with Jane Hamrick and Sue Murner attended the inaugural meeting of the New Baptist Covenant held in Atlanta spearheaded by former president Jimmy Carter and former SBC president the Rev. Dr. Jimmy Allen. Although we are all members of First Baptist Church of Charleston, we attended as individuals. It was thrilling to be among 15,000 other Baptists with such diverse backgrounds seeking common ground. I needed this meeting. Speaker after speaker reminded us of the great heritage we share as Baptists. It renewed my commitments to our historic Baptists principles. I left Atlanta with a greater sense of community.

Carol and I were in Plains, Georgia on March 7, 2010 to hear Jimmy Carter teach Sunday school. Here is a man who is on the world stage and yet holds firm to his convictions. Jimmy Carter is not ashamed to share his faith. He remains humble and gracious. We gladly had our picture taken with him and Rosalyn. He is an outstanding example of what it means to be a Christian. His life exemplifies the meaning of "Our Father." We tried unsuccessfully to get him as a speaker for the Hamrick Lectureship in Charleston, but this opportunity was an outstanding consolation prize.

London and St. Paul's Cathedral are light years away from Woodruff, South Carolina, and Northside Baptist Church, but each is an essential mile marker on a journey—a journey to discover a fuller understanding of who God really is and how I can be more like him. In the process, God revealed a much broader plan for me. He wanted to open my eyes and mind to see who his children are. It is as if he is saying, "Mitch, you can't understand me without knowing and loving my children, your sisters and brothers. I am the Father of all." He is constantly reminding me that I am one of his children and that I belong to a family that is much larger, much more diverse, and much more inclusive than I imagined at the start of my journey.

There are no shutouts in God's family, or as Dr. John Hamrick says, "People are not throw-aways." We all belong. Just as my aunt tried to do fifty years ago, someone or some group is always trying to exclude some other group from God's family for reasons of their own. It never works. You and I are members of the family. We are loved, but we are not the head of the family. That is the basis of all sin—wanting to take the place of God. God is the head of the family. He alone decides who is in and who is out. His greatest desire is that everyone should be a member of his family. My role as a member of the family is to invite others to join by living a life that is truly reflective of what being a child of God is all about. It is about inclusion, not exclusion. It is about love, not hate. It is about accepting the invitation, "Come and learn of me."

14

Autumn

HERE I AM AT 80 years of age trying to put the seemingly unrelated experiences of my life together. During this writing, terrorists struck the World Trade Center and the Pentagon, forcing me to continue the struggle of identifying my core beliefs. Dr. Hamrick, Abbot Kline, David Redd, and Dr. Motter are with God. Our discussion group has changed from monthly to weekly and has greatly expanded to include even more diverse viewpoints. One of those was the Rev. Paul Pridgen Jr., a pioneer in starting the Baptist/ Catholic dialogue. Paul also has joined that heavenly throng far earlier than we would have chosen. He was light years ahead of his time and paid a heavy price for his ecumenicalism. No major Baptist church invited him to guest preach after he retired. His son delivered a masterful eulogy to a packed church. Bob Boston, a retired Presbyterian minister, chaplain, and counselor, has added great depth. He and I were classmates at Furman. Bruce Jane, retired Baptist minister, chaplain, and counselor, is very active in programs dealing with the eradication of the forces that keep people in poverty. Carl Tolbert, retired Baptist minister and chaplain, is deeply involved with the First Christian Church/ Disciples of Christ. John Hughes, also a Furman University alumni, spent twenty-five years as minister of First Baptist Church in Independence, Missouri. John is the interim pastor of First Christian Church/Disciples of Christ. Our wives sometimes join us. Carol Hughes is an ordained Baptist minister. It pains me to look at this list and to think of the talent that is lost to the Southern Baptist Convention. I am the only one who is still a member of a Southern Baptist church. I could not have stayed except for the wonderful culture and love of First Baptist Church of Charleston. It is a truly amazing, warm, accepting, supporting congregation.

I have relished the opportunity to write devotionals for *Reflections*, a publication of the Cooperative Baptist Fellowship, over the last eleven years and *Open Windows, a* Southern Baptist publication. These assignments prompt a great deal of study and soul searching. I am grateful for the opportunity to do what is really a joy for me. Don Kirkland, editor of the bi-weekly (now monthly) *South Carolina Baptist Courier*, asked me to write a series of Sunday school lessons. This was a terrific and challenging learning experience and a high honor. I discovered a wonderful website, www.ethicsdaily.com, and have contributed several essays dealing with Christian communication.

In response to what I believe is God's plan for my life, I launched a campaign to turn down the rhetoric in the Christian community by promoting a Say Something Nice Sunday on the first Sunday in June each year, and editing and contributing to a book featuring a diverse group of Christian leaders, *Christian Civility in an Uncivil World*. Carol did a marvelous job helping me edit these essays. There is a wonderful ecumenical committee working on the Say Something Nice Sunday project, and we have received endorsements from First Baptist Church, the Charleston Baptist Association, the Charleston-Atlantic Presbytery, South Carolina Baptist Convention, Asbury St James Methodist Church, several Episcopal churches, some Lutheran churches, and the Charleston Catholic Diocese, which covers all of South Carolina. The latest endorsement came from Archbishop Dolan of New York just before he became Cardinal Dolan. Many other individual churches have joined to promote the event. In 2014, the Baptist World Alliance agreed to help promote the event.

I think working to improve the quality of Christian communication is God's plan for my life because my life experiences, education, and career have uniquely prepared me for such a role.

The contributors to *Christian Civility in an Uncivil World* came together so readily. The Say Something Nice Sunday Movement is on a steady growth pattern. Thanks to the generous spirit of Pat and Ernest (Bud) Brown, resident hosts, I have led several Brown Bag Lunch discussions on Christian Civility at Baptist House at the Chautauqua Institution.

Carol and I are facing perhaps our most difficult challenge yet. She has been diagnosed with mild to moderate neurological dysfunction. She is no longer able to drive or sing in her beloved Sanctuary Choir at First Baptist Church. Our future is certainly up in the air. We press on, knowing that the God who has brought us safely this far did not bring us here to forsake us now. I pray constantly for guidance and patience.

Where have all of these experiences, large and small, led me? One thing I know is that my spiritual journey continues to evolve. I know that my concept of God is far too small and far too provincial.

I believe that God is love and that He loves all of His children equally and without reservations, including the terrorists.

I believe that our acts of commission or omission that harm each other or that damage our planet interfere with our relationship with God.

I believe that Jesus came to help us understand the nature of God and to reconcile us to God and that my personal reconciliation is through him.

I believe that many paths lead to God and that we see God revealed every day through the lives of others. Peter Gomes expressed this point in his sermon, "Christmas Day." "The miracle of Christmas is that God cared enough to send the very best and that he continues to do so in the gifts now given to us in one another."[1]

I believe that the Kingdom of God is within us and that we do not need to wait for death to experience it.

I believe that a relationship with God is personal, intimate, and life changing.

---

1. Gomes, *Christmas Day: The House of Bread*, 25.

Our Father

I believe that God continues to reveal himself/herself to us, as we are able to understand and experience the revelations. The admonition, "Come and learn of me," is a call to a continuous process of study, reflection, meditation, faith, surrender, and practice (Matt. 11:29 KJV). As the Scriptures exhort us, we are to seek God with all our hearts.

I believe that we encounter God in hundreds of ways every day and that God brings people and experiences into our lives when they are most needed by us.

In short, I know in whom I have believed, and I want to know God more fully.

As I stood in St. Paul's Cathedral experiencing the joy of praying with people from around the world, I had no inkling where the insights gained in that experience would lead me. I only knew that my life would never be the same again, that my comfortable faith had been challenged, and that God was beckoning me to learn more, experience more, love more, trust more, risk more, and to open my heart, my eyes, my ears, my brain, and my soul. I knew that my concept of God was far too inadequate and far too provincially conceived. The insights and the blessings just keep coming. It is an astounding journey. I have no idea where God is leading me or what he might yet reveal. It is disquieting to re-examine, to challenge, and to sometimes give up earlier cherished notions, but the God I am following has called me by name and I am his. I know that he has planed only good for me. "My cup runneth over" (Ps. 23:5 KJV). My quest is to learn and follow what God is calling me to do or be in the autumn of my life.

Bibliography

Allen, James. *As a Man Thinketh*. Westwood, NJ: Revell, n.d., ca. 1902.
Brissie, Sam C. *One Man in His Time*. New York: Carlton, 1983.
Galloway, Dale E. *Expect a Miracle*. Wheaton: Tyndale House, 1982.
Gomes, Peter. *Christmas Day*. New York: Morrow, 1998.
Hall, J. Lincoln. *Songs of faith and triumph*. Philadelphia: Hall-Mack, 1929, "Sunrise," composed by William C. Poole (lyrics) and B.D. Ackley (music), 1924.
Kidd, Pam. *Daily Guidepost*. New York: Daily Guidepost, 2001.
MacDonald, Gordon. "What I Want To Be When I Grow Up." *Leadership* (Fall 1992).
"Optimist Creed." *Optimist International. www.optimist.org/creed.cfm* (8 March, 2015).
"Saint Augustine Quotes." *Brainy Quotes*. http://www.brainyquote.com/quotes/authors/s/saint_augustine.html (12 March 2015).
Schweitzer, Albert. *The Quest of the Historical Jesus*. New York: McMillan, 1961.
Walker, Scott. *Understanding Christianity?: Looking Through the Windows of God*. Macon: Smyth & Helwys, 1992.

www.ingramcontent.com/pod-product-compliance
Lightning Source LLC
Chambersburg PA
CBHW070509090426
42735CB00012B/2709